A Shell Guide

COUNTY DURHAM

IN SHABBY STREETS

Coronation Day 1937

Shildon, Spennymoor, Shiney Row,
  Pelaw, Pity Me, Seldom Seen,
What have you got to-day to show,
  What have you done for your King and Queen?

The flags are flimsy, the streets are shabby,
  With mean low houses of cold grey stone;
But which of the guests that throng the Abbey
  Paid for his flag with a meal foregone?

Paper streamers and cheapest cotton—
  Sign enough for the world to know
That you in London are not forgotten
  In Shildon, Spennymoor, Shiney Row.

Would you choose the Mall with its crowns and gilding,
  If you were King, or if you were Queen,
Or a paper flag on a lonely building
  In Pelaw, Pity Me, Seldom Seen?

                                        C. A. Alington

TO JOHN PIPER
exiguum pignus

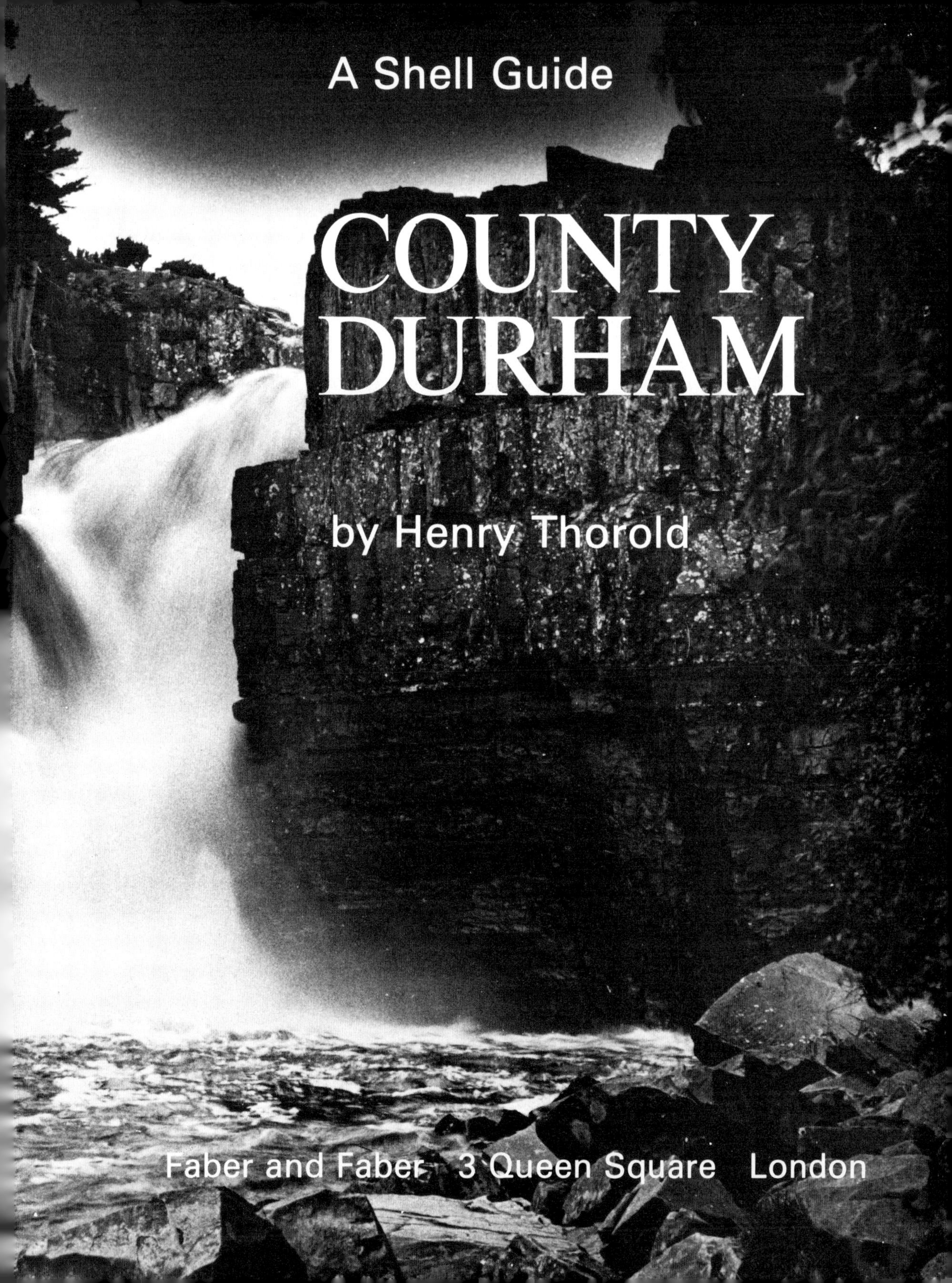

A Shell Guide

COUNTY DURHAM

by Henry Thorold

Faber and Faber 3 Queen Square London

First published in 1980
by Faber and Faber Limited
3 Queen Square London WC1N 3AU
Set, printed and bound in Great Britain by
Fakenham Press Limited
Fakenham, Norfolk

Although sponsoring this book, Shell U.K. Ltd would
point out that the author is expressing his own views.

Replica of Locomotion No. 1 at **Beamish**

British Library Cataloguing in Publication Data

Thorold, Henry
  County Durham. – (A Shell guide).
  1. Durham, Eng. (County) – Description and
travel – Guide-books
  I. Title   II. Series
  914.28′6′04857   DA670.D9
  ISBN 0–571–11640–X

Acknowledgements

In 1974 I was completing *The Shell Guide to Staffordshire*: I was enthusing to Mr John Piper, Editor of the *Shell Guides*, about Staffordshire, about maligned counties. 'Maligned counties?' he said, 'you'd better do County Durham next.' Great gratitude to him for this: great gratitude to him too, and to Mr Edward Piper, for their help and their photographs.

And grateful thanks to other friends: Mr Mervyn James, of the University of Durham, entertained me often at Leazes Place, and took me on my first tours of the county; Mr T. H. Summerson entertained me at Coatham Mundeville; Mrs Pennyman at Ormesby Hall, providing me from a bedroom window in Yorkshire with one of the finest panoramic views of County Durham; Mr William Whitfield entertained me at that most remarkable house, St Helen Hall; Mr John Stevens-Guille, Mr John Barratt, and the Revd Basil Wilks (with his camera) accompanied me on many expeditions. Mrs C. F. Battiscombe (Georgina Battiscombe) lent me a shelf-ful of Durham books; Mr Neville Whittaker introduced me to the delights of Durham buildings through his *Historic Architecture of County Durham* (Oriel Press, 1971), and subsequently on many occasions in the county; Sir Jasper More once again assisted me with railway history; Lady Home of the Hirsel has kindly allowed me to reproduce the poem on page 1, by her father, the late Dean of Durham. I am also most grateful to Lord and Lady Barnard, the Dowager Lady Barnard, Sir John Eden, Bt., M.P., the Revd Gerard Irvine, Mr and Mrs R. A. Morritt, and the late Dowager Lady Scarbrough.

The Shell Guide to County Durham (in common with other volumes in the series) treats of the historic County of Durham, which stretches from the Tees to the Tyne. But, for convenience, the book also includes the few parishes south of the Tees, at present annexed to County Durham.

Marston Hall,
Lincolnshire   HENRY THOROLD
July 1980

List of Illustrations

Note: Captions to the photographs include place names in **bold type.** These refer to entries in the gazetteer, pages 47–187.

7

Introduction

County Durham: its very title is unique. Yorkshire — Northumberland — Lancashire —Lincolnshire—Sussex—Dorset—Rutland —but *County* Durham. There are echoes of Ireland, suggestions of a domain not quite English, of something a trifle outlandish: *County* Durham.

And County Durham is unique. For much of its history it has been a domain on its own, not quite like the rest of England, a County Palatine, the Prince Bishoprick. County Durham is a trifle outlandish, a trifle odd among English counties; and herein lies its charm.

County Durham is a world apart: it is protected on the south by the great River

◁ Farms on **Stanhope** Common (*top*) and near **Rookhope**

▽ Hedley Hill near **Esh Winning**

The moorland landscape: *p12* Lunedale (*top*) and near **Middleton-in-Teesdale**; *p13* Above Cauldron Snout, Upper Teesdale ▷

The Tees at Middleton-one-Row (*see* **Middleton St George**)...

Tees, on the north by the great River Tyne, on the east by the cold North Sea. And on the west? On the west no doubt there is a frontier, somewhere in those great wild moorlands which it shares with Cumberland and Westmorland—but one likes to think that the western frontier is still disputed territory, where the army of the Prince Bishop guards its remote borders, making a sortie here, a sally there, to maintain its territorial rights against invaders, even though the armies now are but flocks of sheep, grazing those desolate lands, and the invaders are but intrepid walkers or determined climbers.

How to see County Durham

For the explorer from the south, from England, the ideal place to enter County Durham is Piercebridge, where a stately 18th-century bridge crosses the River Tees. Just past Scotch Corner turn left; ignore the motorway which will whisk a foolish, hasty traveller through the length of the Palatinate in thirty minutes and land him in Newcastle, showing him nothing on the way, not even allowing him to see the cathedral as the railway does in its grand panoramic sweep past Durham City. No, turn left, and take that old straight Roman road. From the vantage

... and at **Piercebridge**

point here is the first sight of the spreading hills of County Durham—so different from the hills of Yorkshire: the sense of excitement grows. And just before the bridge at Piercebridge is the George, that admirable hostelry just in Yorkshire. From the windows of the dining room is the perfect view of the Tees, tumbling, bubbling on its way. And the farther bank is County Durham.

We can cross the river, and enter the Palatinate. Piercebridge village is typical of County Durham—quite different from a Yorkshire village. A long rectangular green, with terraces of one-storeyed cottages, and a small Victorian church with a bell-cote. It might almost be in Scotland. Behind the village are the excavated remains of a Roman fort—again so typical of County Durham. Look at the map: Binchester, Lanchester, Ebchester—and the great fort at the mouth of the Tyne, at South Shields. There are deep Roman roots in County Durham.

From Piercebridge the straight road carries on—then turns left and abruptly descends, descends from exhilarating rural countryside into the industrial village of West Auckland. The transformation is sudden: a worked-out colliery, newer

15

above and opposite (*top*) **Gainford**

factories. But, again, it is a village with a long green. Apparently these villages with their enclosed greens date back to the times of the Scottish raids: the flocks of sheep and herds of cattle could be driven in to graze—and so avoid falling prey to the marauders. So industry begins, and takes over: West Auckland, St Helen Auckland, Bishop Auckland; factories, trading estates, worked-out collieries; Spennymoor—more factories, more trading estates, more worked-out collieries; and so to Durham itself.

Durham on its peninsula, its steep well-wooded banks washed by the River Wear, is supreme. The cathedral is the grandest Norman church in Europe; the city, with its cobbled streets and secret walks, its castle and its university, has unique presence.

The ideal time to see Durham is December. The crowds who come in summer will be gone: the place will belong to its citizens and academics once more. The cathedral is never more beautiful than at Evensong on Advent Sunday: we go in in daylight—during the service we see the daylight fade, and the cathedral becomes dark.

16

Sedgefield

Headlam (*top*)
Piercebridge

Langton near **Ingleton**
Near **Middleton-in-Teesdale**

Durham from below the station

The College ▷

To the accompaniment of solemn Advent music we can watch the shadows lengthen—and walk out into darkness. The cathedral will be flood-lit—so will the castle. The castle, so long the great fortress of the Prince Bishops, whom the Conqueror set up to rule the Palatinate, the semi-independent kingdom, a bulwark to protect Northern England from the Scots: here the Bishops ruled until 1836, enacting their own laws, minting their own money, levying their own taxes, and raising their own army. The lights on Palace Green will illuminate 18th-century houses, and older and newer buildings of the university. We can walk down to the river below the Galilee, up again into College Green to the south of the cathedral, see the houses of the canons—and so through South Bailey and North Bailey, one long string of captivating houses, big and small, back into the outside world. Next day, in daylight, on a crisp winter morning perhaps, we can visit Prebends' Bridge and South Street, see the cathedral across the Wear, and visit the castle—the castle given by the last Prince Bishop, van Mildert, in

1832 to the newly founded university—see the Hall, now the Hall of University College, see Cosin's Black Staircase and the Bishops' former State Apartments, now the Senior Common Room of the college.

Durham, indeed, has few rivals.

Durham City is, of course, the ideal place from which to make expeditions to the four corners of the Principality. To the Tyne, to see Gateshead, now ruined by monstrous tower-blocks, an ancient town now desecrated by 'relief roads', dual carriageways, roundabouts, underpasses, flyovers: a concrete jungle indeed. To see Felling, Heworth, Hebburn, the Tyne shipyards, Jarrow, South Shields. Or to go west to see Blaydon, Stella, and a great house, Axwell Park, by James Paine, now almost submerged by modern housing, with the great chimneys of a coking works belching smoke at its gates. To see Ryton, and another 18th-century house, perhaps by Paine, Bradley Hall—an incredible oasis still surrounded by its park. Or to go south to visit Gibside, and follow the course of the Derwent to Hunstanworth, the church and village built by Teulon on the edge of the moors.

Another tour could take us to Sunderland, to see Monkwearmouth with its Saxon church and grandest of early railway stations, the mouth of the Wear, an old dockland community, and the beautiful and intriguing 19th-century residential development of Ashbrook, to see E. S. Prior's masterpiece, Roker church. Further south along the coast is Seaham, that sad and slightly comic little harbour, built by the 3rd Marquis of Londonderry for his coal, and Horden Hall, a perfect early 17th-century manor house almost submerged by the vast collieries at Blackhall.

A little further south is Hartlepool, with its great Early English church, relics of mediaeval town walls, and little early 19th-century sea-front houses—which might almost be in Brighton. West Hartlepool is the mid-Victorian dockland town; and south again is Seaton Carew, a curious faded little seaside resort, a north country version of, perhaps, Littlehampton. And so to Billingham, home of I.C.I., to Stockton, and the mouth of the Tees. Inland from here is Wynyard, the great early 19th-century palace of Lord Londonderry: further inland still is Sedgefield, a little ancient market town.

Another tour could take us due south to Darlington, where we can worship at the shrine of the earliest railway—at North Road Station, now a railway museum—and again at the splendid, later, Bank Top Station. Darlington is an ancient town, which preserves some of the air of an old market town, with Waterhouse's Market Hall, and with a glorious Early English church. Not far away is Shildon, another historic railway town, where the first passenger train in the world was set on its way in 1825.

Or we can go west from Durham, to Ushaw College, the great Roman Catholic seminary, redolent of Pugin, and on to Lanchester, to Wolsingham, to Stanhope, and up the valley of the Wear—to mile after endless mile of desolate moorland, some of the wildest country in England. This was the ancient home of lead mining, and at Killhope we can see the great wheel, used for crushing lead. Further south is Middleton-in-Teesdale, and a short distance up the river are those magnificent waterfalls, Cauldron Snout and High Force.

The valley of the Tees is magical, with unspoiled and unsophisticated villages: Gainford, Staindrop, Winston, Whorlton, and the ancient market town of Barnard

St Paul's, **Jarrow**, and the monastery

Castle, the countryside marked out by the whitewashed farms of the Raby estate. South of the river is that jewel of a house, that irresistible prize, Sir Thomas Robinson's Rokeby; next door is mediaeval Mortham Tower. And not far away is Wycliffe, birthplace of John Wycliffe. A fragment of the mediaeval manor house is incorporated in the serene and beautiful 18th-century house, standing high up on the south bank of the Tees. Here the visitor may choose to stay:

there are few more delectable spots in all England than Greta Bridge.

Round Durham itself we could do a tour of old pit villages—where odd, ugly rows of miners' cottages climb the hills, and drab Victorian churches and little public houses keep them company. But villages they are—villages with the oddest names: Shiney Row, Sunnyside, Quaking Houses, Quebec, Toronto, Philadelphia, Pity Me!—the countryside begins where the last miners'

St Peter's, Monkwearmouth (*see* **Sunderland**)

terrace ends; County Durham is not one vast, built-up, industrial area. Indeed, as we drive along the hilly roads around the city, wide and unexpected landscapes constantly open up; and nearer the coast—in Georgina Battiscombe's words—'those steep, secretive denes, so characteristic of the Durham countryside, wind their way down to the coal-blackened sea'.

It is in these surroundings that unexpected treasures lie.

Architecture: churches

The little Saxon churches are the special glory of County Durham. 'To St Peter's Church, A.D. 675' reads a signpost in industrial Sunderland; 'To St Paul's Monastery, A.D. 684', another signpost in a jungle of new roads on the edge of a desolate swamp at Jarrow. Both churches suffered subsequent depredations, both received 19th-century additions—but these ancient shrines are very precious. And at Escomb, near Bishop

Brancepeth △

◁ Cosin screens at **Sedgefield**

Auckland, is a complete little Saxon church of much the same date—complete with narrow lofty nave, and narrow chancel arch leading into narrow lofty chancel. This indeed is a moving little church.

Other early churches come to mind: Norton, now a pretty suburb of Stockton, with its Saxon and early Norman crossing tower; Billingham, almost engulfed by I.C.I., with another early tower; Pittington with its unique arcade, perhaps inspired by the Galilee at Durham. There are those early

crosses at St Andrew Auckland and at Kelloe.

St Hilda's at Hartlepool is a great 13th-century church, with an extraordinary heavily buttressed west tower, overlooking its cliffs and its harbour; St Cuthbert's at Darlington is a grand town church of much the same date, with lancets and arcading of rare refinement. At Finchale, in a quiet tree-hung bend of the River Wear north of Durham are the remains of church and monastic buildings of the 13th-century

27

St Andrew's, Roker (*see* **Sunderland**)

Benedictine Priory. At Chester-le-Street, at Gainford, at Houghton-le-Spring, at Lanchester and Staindrop, are notable churches of many dates: West Boldon boasts an early broach spire, Ryton an important lead-covered spire, reminiscent of Long Sutton. Spires are rare in County Durham.

But something unique to County Durham is the 'Cosin' woodwork: at Sedgefield, at Brancepeth, in the Chapel at Auckland Castle, at Haughton-le-Skerne and Gateshead, at Easington and St Mary-le-Bow in Durham is this unique 17th-century church furnishing to be found: screens and stalls and pews, all of unparalleled richness, either introduced, or inspired, by Bishop Cosin after the Restoration. Partly mediaeval in detail, partly Renaissance, there is nothing like it anywhere else in England.

At Sunderland and Stockton are imposing 18th-century town churches; James Paine built the rare private chapel and mausoleum of the Bowes family at Gibside. And so to the 19th century.

Gilbert Scott? Street? Butterfield? Bodley? There is little to see of their work—though Scott restored the cathedral, and Pearson was born in the county. There is a minor

28

Gibside chapel

church by Street at Frosterley, a minor church by Butterfield at Belmont, and a minor church by Pearson at Darlington. There is Christ Church at West Hartlepool by E. B. Lamb, and Hunstanworth (with its village) by Teulon. Otherwise we look to local architects: Pickering of Sunderland, with his neo-Norman churches at Birtley and St Mary-the-Less, Durham; Pritchett of Darlington with his monumental Presbyterian church at Sunderland; Hodgson Fowler at St Columba's, Southwick, and St Ignatius's, Sunderland; and William Searle Hicks with his masterpieces at St Chad's,

Gateshead, and St Oswald's, Hartlepool—two churches which seem too little known. In many a mining village there was too little money to build anything but the barest Victorian church.

In a paragraph to itself must be St Andrew's, Roker, by E. S. Prior—with furnishings by Burne-Jones, William Morris, E. W. Gimson and Eric Gill.

p30 **Pelton** (*top*) and **Tow Law**; *p31* St Andrew's Presbyterian, **Hebburn-on-Tyne** (*top*) and St Chad's, **Gateshead** ▷

29

Castles and houses

Raby is the perfect mediaeval castle, 'improved' by Carr of York in the 18th century, by Burn in the 19th; Lumley stands four-square, built by a Lumley in the 14th century, and still held by a Lumley—glorified by Vanbrugh in the early 18th century. Brancepeth was done up in the 1820s and 1830s by John Patterson of Edinburgh for Matthew Russell, who was brother-in-law to Charles Tennyson-d'Eyncourt who built Bayons Manor in Lincolnshire: no doubt they egged each other on. Auckland Castle, part mediaeval, part Bishop Cosin, part James Wyatt, is the most magnifical Bishop's Palace in England.

As for the later houses of County Durham, who has ever heard of them? Of Walworth Castle, near the Tees, another Lulworth, of 1600; of Gainford Hall, a 'Smythsonian' manor house of 1603; of Biddick, that distinguished little Vanbrugian house of 1720, or of Croxdale of 1760, where the Salvins have lived since the early 15th century? Who knows of Elemore with its plasterwork, in a deep valley close to pits, or of St Helen Hall, standing close to the road near Bishop Auckland, that house containing the finest 18th-century rooms in the county, miraculously rescued by Mr William Whitfield in recent years?

In a final paragraph must be mentioned the 19th-century palace of the Londonderrys at Wynyard, the great former Eden house at Windlestone, and Burn Hall, a former Salvin house, both by Bonomi, both of c. 1830.

Towns

As for towns, there are delightsome 18th-century streets in Durham and Barnard Castle, and fragments of good terraces in Stockton and Sunderland. Of the early 19th century, modest seaside housing is to be found at Hartlepool and Seaton Carew; later in the century the remarkable development of Ashbrook, that leafy suburb of Sunderland, occurred; there are also some agreeable terraces in Darlington. There are 18th-century town halls at South Shields, at Stockton and at Barnard Castle—and the Bowes Museum and the South Shields Municipal Buildings are both breathtaking creations of the turn of the 19th century.

The University of Durham

After Oxford and Cambridge, Durham is the oldest university in England. Twice, in earlier centuries, attempts were made to establish a university at Durham, first under Henry VIII when a scheme was proposed for founding a university college from the funds of the dissolved monasteries; again under Cromwell, when in 1657 letters patent were issued for the foundation of a collegiate body to be known as 'The Provost, Fellows and Scholars of the College in Durham'. Both schemes came to naught.

But in 1832 Bishop van Mildert, the last Prince Bishop, realizing that after his death the Palatinate would be abolished and its powers and endowments transferred to the Crown, persuaded the Dean and Chapter to found the university, to which a portion of the ecclesiastical funds would be surrendered. He himself bequeathed the Castle, one of the two episcopal palaces of the See, and £2,000 a year out of his income, to the new foundation. The first undergraduates came into residence in 1833 in Bishop Cosin's Hall (then known as Archdeacon's Inn). Soon afterwards the Castle became University College.

Raby Castle (*top*) ▷

Brancepeth Castle

32

△ Biddick Hall (see **Lambton**)

▽ Lumley Castle (see **Chester-le-Street**)

Gainford Hall (*top*);

St Helen Hall, **St Helen Auckland** ▷

The original scheme was based on the idea of Christ Church, Oxford, with the Dean as Head of the College, and the Canons as Professors; this did not actually materialize, but two Canons are university professors. A second college, Hatfield, was founded in 1846, St Chad's in 1904 and St John's in 1909. Since then, the number of colleges and societies has increased to fourteen. With its colleges and university buildings—and its bookshops—Durham, alone in England, shares with Oxford and Cambridge the air and character of a university town.

Industry

The landscape of the county has been shaped by industry. Lead mining in Weardale—where the awesome wheel at Killhope stands as a memorial to the trade; shipbuilding on the Tyne, at Hebburn and Jarrow, and on the Wear at Sunderland; harbours at South Shields and Sunderland, at Seaham and Hartlepool; the great chemical works at Billingham, at the mouth of the Tees—all these have shaped the county. But coal has dominated all.

Coal has been worked in the Principality for centuries—in a small way, perhaps, by the Romans, certainly after the Conquest on a larger scale, for the Boldon Book alludes to 'carbones' on the properties of the Prince Bishops, and opencast mining is known to have taken place in the 12th century. The development continued slowly: coal was dug from the banks of the Tyne in the 13th century, from the Wear in the 14th. In 1350 a mine was opened at Coundon, and soon after at Lumley and Cockfield. Soon the Prince

Seaham Harbour

◁ Souterpoint lighthouse, **South Shields**

Bishops were selling mining rights all over the Principality: the coal was carried to the staiths on the rivers, and so transported by sea, from Sunderland or South Shields, to London. At Gateshead, at Whickham, at Stella and Ravensworth: here the valuable deposits were worked.

By the 18th century every landowner who had the good fortune to own coal was working his pits. The 'Grand Allies'—Russells of Brancepeth, Liddells of Ravensworth, Strathmores of Gibside—between them owned the best pits in the north; the Hedworths, the Lambtons, and the Lumleys owned valuable mines near Chester-le-Street; the Three Baronets (Milbanke, Blake and Thorold) worked their pits near Houghton-le-Spring. The Dean and Chapter had their tremendous mine near Ferryhill.

But in the 19th century the coming of the railways revolutionized the coal industry: new deep mines in east Durham were sunk and developed, and Lord Londonderry built Seaham Harbour to transport his coal from the enormous pits at Rainton. All over the north and east of the county hideous little mining villages were built, and the landscape of the county was scarred by slag heaps. Most of these have now been flattened; new industries have been imported to fill the vacuum where the worked-out pits have closed. Today the great mines along the coast, and far out to sea, represent the coal of County Durham. But though many pits are dead, the coal industry—and its attendant litter—still dominates the county.

Railways

Durham, with its rolling hills and deep valleys, was unsuitable for canals—though Jeremiah Dixon of Cockfield made plans for a canal system in the neighbourhood of

△ Opencast coal near **Esh Winning**

▽ Mined coal at **Beamish**

Abandoned lead mine at Killhope (*see* **Cowshill**) (*top*)
Shipbuilding at Monkwearmouth (*see* **Sunderland**)

▷

△ **Stanley**

▽ **Tow Law**

Bishop Auckland ▷

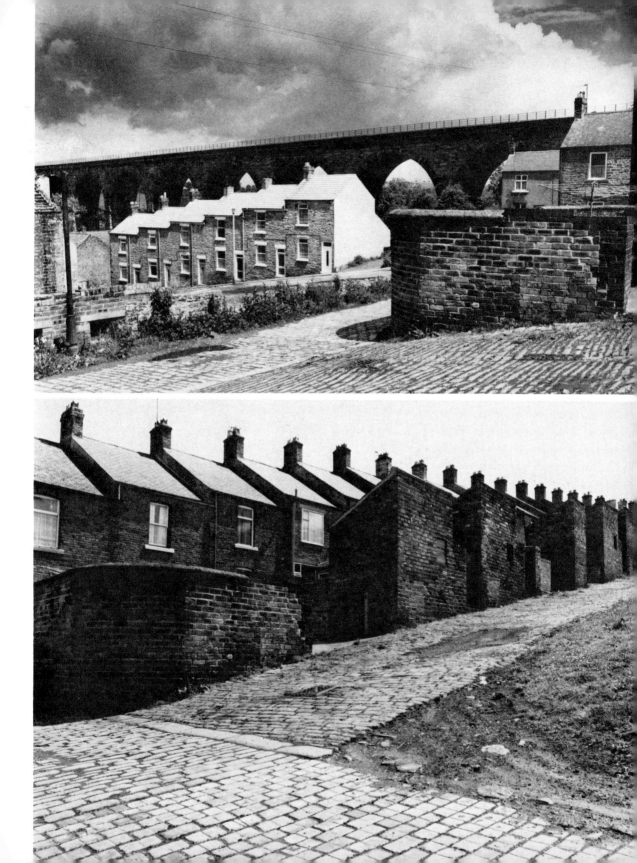

Monkwearmouth Station

Hamsterley viaduct

Cockfield and Etherley, and his plans survive in the possession of a descendant. However, it was County Durham that gave railways to the world, and—thanks to Edward Pease and Jonathan Backhouse, and their engineer George Stephenson—the first public railway in the world was opened when Locomotion N° 1 drew a train-load of passengers and coal from Shildon to Darlington and Stockton on 27 September 1825, and the Stockton and Darlington Railway was born.

Great railway viaducts span the county—at Consett, at Hamsterley on the Derwent, at Penshaw and at Durham itself. There are great Victorian railway stations at Darlington (Bank Top) and at Stockton, as well as the charming North Road Station at Darlington and the imposing neo-Classical station at Monkwearmouth—both of which are now impressive railway museums. For the railway enthusiast there are also the Open Air Museum at Beamish and the Timothy Hackworth Museum at

42

Shildon—Shildon, holy ground to all lovers of trains.

Celebrities

A great cavalcade of distinguished men and women have been either born in, or closely associated with the county. In the world of art, literature and science, Thomas Wright (1710–86), astronomer, was born at Byers Green; George Dixon (1731–85), inventor of coal gas, and his brother Jeremiah (1733–79), astronomer, were born at Cockfield; William Shield (1748–1829), composer and Master of the King's Musick, was born at Whickham; Robert Surtees (1779–1834), antiquary, was born at Mainsforth; Robert Smith Surtees (1803–64), author, and creator of Jorrocks, was born at Hamsterley; Elizabeth Barrett Browning (1806–61), poet, was born at Coxhoe; John Loughborough Pearson (1817–97), architect, was born at Durham; and Gertrude Bell (1868–1926), archaeologist and explorer, was born at Washington. Anthony Salvin (1799–1881), architect, though not born in the county, belonged to one of its most ancient families, and worked extensively in the county; John Bacchus Dykes (1823–76), hymnologist, was for many years Precentor of the Cathedral and Vicar of St Oswald's; and John Meade Falkner (1858–1932), author, lived for many years on Palace Green as Hon. Librarian to the Dean and Chapter.

In the world of politics, John George Lambton, 1st Earl of Durham (1792–1840), statesman and Governor-General of Canada, was born at Lambton; and Sir Anthony Eden, 1st Earl of Avon (1897–1977), Prime Minister, was born at Windlestone. Two other Prime Ministers, though not natives, for many years held parliamentary seats in the county: Ramsay MacDonald (1866–1937), Member for Seaham; and Harold Macmillan (1894–), Member for Stockton. Lord Shinwell (1884–), Member for Easington, and Lord Dalton (1877–1961), Member for Bishop Auckland, though again not natives, may be mentioned among prominent politicians closely associated with County Durham.

Of Durham soldiers, General Sir Henry Havelock (1797–1857), saviour of Lucknow, was born at Bishopwearmouth; his son General Sir Henry Havelock-Allan, V.C. (1830–97), was born at Darlington; and Field Marshal Viscount Gort, V.C. (1886–1946), Commander-in-Chief of the British Land Forces, was born at Hamsterley.

In addition to all these, a number of remarkable men have held the See of Durham since the Reformation—and a few of these, though not natives, must be mentioned in the Roll of Honour: splendid characters of the 17th century, such as John Cosin (1594–1672), beautifier and restorer of the Bishoprick after the Civil War; and Nathaniel, Lord Crewe (1633–1721), great benefactor of the Bishoprick and of Oxford University; of the 18th century, Joseph Butler (1692–1752), theologian and philosopher; Victorian scholars and apostles such as Joseph Barber Lightfoot (1828–89) and Brooke Foss Westcott (1825–1901); and in our own time that man of wit and independence, Herbert Hensley Henson (1863–1947). Such are a few of the men who have ruled the Bishoprick.

County Durham: the Palatinate: the Prince Bishoprick: the Patrimony of St Cuthbert; home of the Venerable Bede, and other early northern saints: as we make our way north from Durham towards the Tyne and survey that scarred, industrialized,

The **Penshaw** Monument

northern half of the county, we see in the background that blackened Northern Parthenon, the Penshaw Monument, erected in 1844 to the memory of the 1st Earl of Durham, 'Radical Jack', 'King Jog', local hero—erected on the hill where his ancestor, an early Lambton, fought the legendary monster, the Lambton Worm. There it stands, a landmark for miles around, symbolic of the county—a county that is rugged but endearing, tough but charming, aristocratic and plebeian, over-run yet unknown, maligned but magnificent.

This independent, individual county will not disappoint the discerning, the determined, explorer.

Gazetteer

The number in brackets following the place name refers to the square on the map at the back of the book where the place is to be found.

Annfield Plain [4] A satellite of Stanley. *St Aidan's* is a plain brick church of 1914 at the road junction: long terraces survey the view east, part rural, part industrial—with the Morrison Busty Coal Preparation Plant prominent to the south.

Auckland, Bishop [10] The approach from the south is disappointing and dismal: the road from St Helen Auckland is littered with factories and cheap housing—though at the traffic lights, at the entrance to the town, it is possible to catch a glimpse of the tower of *St Andrew Auckland* or South Church, the ancient parish church of Bishop Auckland. The main street comprises dull shops, punctuated by a strange succession of seemingly endless late Victorian or early 20th-century Nonconformist chapels. And so one enters the market place. From the north-west the approach is more promising, over the 15th-century *Newton Cap Bridge* which here crosses the River Wear—the Wear bordering the town on the north and west, as the little River Gaunless does on the east. But the best approach is from the north, along the minor road

◁ The Gatehouse, **Bishop Auckland** Castle

▽   The Bishop's apartments beyond the screen

from Willington, through Binchester. The last mile runs close to the bank of the Wear, and along this road there is a rewarding view of the castle, standing on its high ground above the river. All roads lead into the *market place*—and to arrive here is indeed an experience. The centre of the square is occupied by a most unexpected group of buildings: a tall Victorian *town hall* (of 1869) accompanied by an almost equally tall, narrow, Victorian *parish church* (of 1847). The flèche of the church, the Gothic outline of the town hall, the curious rather cramped site in the middle of the square, combine to give a strange almost French character to the centre of the town—but it is French in a decidedly grim northern way. Even on a sunny day, the square bustling with crowds on market day, there is a dour, sombre

quality about this market place. But to arrive here is an experience. There are two good 18th-century brick houses on the south side of the square; there is *Barclays Bank*, a vintage building of 1870 in brick and stone; the *King's Arms*, with its plain 18th-century stucco front perhaps masking an older core; and in Newgate Street the *Yorkshire Bank*, a small baronial building of 1859. At the east end of the market place the diminutive Castle Square leads to the gatehouse to *Auckland Castle*. Few episcopal, or even archiepiscopal, palaces can compare with Auckland in scale or romance. As we have seen (Introduction p. 20), the Bishops of Durham were no ordinary bishops: they were (until 1836) Prince Bishops, Counts Palatine—the sword of state, crossed with the bishop's crook, the coroneted mitre: these symbols of

their territorial as well as their spiritual power are to be seen throughout the Bishoprick, and especially in their palaces here and at Durham. Since their gift of Durham Castle to their newly founded university in 1832, Auckland has been the seat of the bishops—but indeed it has been their favourite place of residence since the 12th century. The Gothick *gatehouse* is a captivating introduction to the castle: pinnacled and battlemented, with its square clock tower crowned with a large weather vane, it was built about 1750 for Bishop Trevor by Sir Thomas Robinson, amateur architect, squire of Rokeby (q.v.). Past the tall 17th-century *guardhouse* with its mullioned bay windows, the broad drive leads on to the park, lying around and below, where the River Gaunless tumbles

North approach to **Bishop Auckland** (*top*) ▷

The deercote in the Bishop's Park

▽ **Bishop Auckland** town hall and parish church

on its way to join the River Wear. But on the left is James Wyatt's open Gothick screen, which—half-way along—steps back to form a triple-arched battlemented gateway on the axis of the front door, and the drive leads in to the house itself, in its setting of spreading lawns. Stand back on one of these lawns and survey the group of buildings: on the right, most prominent, is the *Chapel*, clerestoried and pinnacled; behind this is the lower connecting wing, which contains the porch and front door; and next—extending L-wise—what might be a Great Hall, with long Gothick windows on its first floor; then a lower wing again, with Tudor windows; finally the south wing, ending in a Gothick bay window facing south. What dates may be assigned to these disparate parts? Little that meets the eye could be assigned to the 12th century; and yet, in fact, the Chapel, so gloriously converted into chapel by Bishop Cosin, is the 12th-century Great Hall, built by Bishop Pudsey with nave and aisles, like Oakham Castle in Rutland. James Wyatt built the connecting wing with porch; James Wyatt redecorated the *State Room* (with the long Gothick windows on the first floor); behind the adjoining Tudor bay are rooms decorated for Bishop Trevor; and the south wing (which contains the Bishop's private apartments) was completed for Trevor's successor, Bishop Egerton, perhaps by Carr of York. It was James Wyatt who was called in by Bishop Barrington in the early 1790s to pull the whole ensemble together. Entering Wyatt's porch and turning left we come to his Gothick entrance hall and Gothick stairs. A window on the landing facing north surveys the wild landscape, scarred with industry; and turning right we approach his *Ante-Room*, vaulted in plaster, richly adorned with Gothick panels, Gothick pilasters, and pinnacled recesses. The double

Bishop Auckland Castle: the King Charles Room...

doors are opened—and at the far end of the State Room is the throne, set below a delicate pinnacled canopy, all in plaster. The room is vaulted—again in plaster—and here hang portraits of many of Durham's greatest bishops: John Cosin, of course, Nathaniel Lord Crewe, Joseph Butler, Richard Trevor, John Egerton, Shute Barrington, William van Mildert, J. B. Lightfoot, Brooke Foss Westcott, Hensley Henson, Michael Ramsey. It is a grand conception: what other Bishop's Palace has a Throne Room? The bones of this great room, the Great Chamber of the

mediaeval house, are of course ancient—as are those of the two rooms adjoining, the *Great Dining Room*, and the *King Charles Room*. Both were redecorated for Bishop Trevor, both have plaster ceilings of the mid-18th century, both are classical in design (for all that they are lighted by Gothick windows—and in the case of the former, by the upper part of the Tudor bay window). The Great Dining Room is hung with the magnificent set of Zurbarans depicting Jacob and the Patriarchs, acquired for the room by Trevor himself. And beyond these two

50

. . . and the Gothick Stairs

rooms lie the Bishop's private apartments. Behind this south wing is a long domestic range extending west, called Scotland (where Scottish prisoners and hostages were quartered, in the days of border raids), and here and beneath the state rooms are the ancient kitchens and offices. But we must return to Wyatt's front door, and enter the *Chapel*. To enter the Chapel is breathtaking—for the great size of the building, the great height, the array of Cosin woodwork, the carved and panelled roof, the memorials to former bishops, all suggest a major collegiate

church rather than a private chapel. The arcades of Bishop Pudsey's hall are lofty in themselves: above them Cosin built the clerestory of seven traceried windows, traceried à la 17th-century Gothic; the roof is decorated with alternating panels depicting the arms of the diocese and the fret of Cosin's arms. The screens and stalls are perhaps the finest examples of Cosin's woodwork, and recall the similar woodwork at Brancepeth, at Sedgefield, and the cathedral itself. Here Cosin was determined to endow a chapel according to the noblest ideals of High Anglican

piety. Only the east end has been changed: Wyatt designed a Gothick reredos for Bishop Barrington, which in turn was replaced by the present altar designed for Bishop Lightfoot by Hodgson Fowler (1884). The stained glass is also of this date. Apart from all this there is at the west end a gallery with a most handsome organ, by Father Smith. It bears the arms of Bishop Lord Crewe, and was his gift. And at the west end of the south aisle is an imposing monument by Nollekens to Bishop Trevor, with a life-size figure of him sitting in his throne. Trevor, who next to Cosin and Barrington did more for Auckland than any other bishop, was nicknamed by George II 'the Beauty of Holiness', and by Horace Walpole 'St Durham'. He has the curious distinction of having been enthroned in his northern cathedral by proxy: he was, in his own right, squire of Glynde in Sussex, where Sir Thomas Robinson built for him that charming little 18th-century church—an almost identical version of the church Sir Thomas built for himself at Rokeby (q.v.). And in the centre of the chapel, in the floor, is the simple black marble slab marking the burial place of John Cosin himself, founder of the chapel. The castle is not open to the public, but the *Bishop's Park* is, and contains a golf course. There is also an 18th-century Gothick *deercote*: quadrangular, with open Gothick arcades and a tower which originally had in its upper floor a banqueting room, it was built for Bishop Trevor perhaps by Carr of York. And along the road to Spennymoor is a pair of decayed but chaste Palladian gate piers, rarely noticed. Could they perhaps betray the hand of Sir Thomas Robinson? Driving into Bishop Auckland from the south there is a sudden glimpse of a venerable church tower along a side road to the east—*St Andrew Auckland*, or South Church, the ancient mother church of Bishop

51

Auckland. Approaching it, the church stands dominatingly above mean houses, in a churchyard raised above the level of the road, a long impressive building, with transepts and two-storeyed porch. It is one of the great churches of County Durham, founded as a collegiate church, and is almost entirely of the late 13th century. Beautiful vaulted porch; long vistaed interior, with the nave of five bays opening out into spacious transepts and chancel beyond. The greatest treasure is the Anglo-Saxon cross (c. 800), reconstructed from fragments discovered during the restoration in 1881. On the base are carved three haloed figures; in the panel above, the Crucifixion; and in the top two figures, one holding a cross: scrolls of foliage with birds and animals adorn the sides. In the chancel is a set of twenty-eight stalls with misericords, the gift of Cardinal Langley. South of the church there has been a great clearance of old houses, and agreeable new houses line the road to Shildon. And visible from the church porch, across the street, and surrounded by unexpected green fields, stand what appear to be the remains of old farm and manorial buildings: a lane leads up to these relics of the old *Deanery*. There is the fragment of a mediaeval house, with spiral staircase and mullioned windows; and there are old barns and buildings around. All is now in the course of restoration. If the church is locked, the key may be found at the Red Alligator opposite.

Auckland, St Helen [10] The approach from Bishop Auckland is terrible: factories, a trading estate, a cash-and-carry store, council houses—the sprawl is unending. Then, as the road bends, an exceptionally grand house suddenly appears, almost on top of the road itself. This is St Helen Auckland: the house St Helen Hall. At first it is difficult to take the house in, standing in this awkward situation: a sublimely beautiful Palladian façade, five great windows on the *piano nobile*, smaller windows on the ground floor, a high-pitched, hipped roof oversailing the cornice; the only adornment is the blind balustrading beneath the first floor windows, and the finely-detailed rustication on the ground floor. It is pure Palladian, perfectly proportioned, reticent, restful. Behind this front, and alongside the road, is an earlier house of three storeys, with mullioned windows and three small gables—for all its three storeys a dwarf beside the rest. Even the casual passer-by cannot fail to be impressed by this unexpected house, nor can he fail to notice the new hedges and plantations that now surround it. John Carr of Newcastle bought property at St Helen in 1610, and soon afterwards, no doubt, built the old wing of the house. In 1731 James's great-granddaughter inherited the place, and soon after married William Carr, M.P. for Newcastle, a man of grand ideas. He was the builder of the Palladian house, and he died in 1741; so it was in the 1730s that this remarkable house was built. Who was the architect? It is a problem that teases architectural historians. James Paine has been suggested—but he would have been too young; Sir Thomas Robinson of Rokeby (q.v.) is a possible contender—he worked at Auckland Castle—as is Daniel Garrett, Lord Burlington's principal draughtsman. Since William Carr's death the property has changed hands often and no building records have come to light as yet. Sir Christopher Musgrave, a Cumberland baronet, bought the place in the 1750s; thereafter it was for a time occupied by Roman Catholic nuns; in the 19th century Joseph Pease, M.P., lived here. There was a succession of different owners, and after the last war the house was in a bad way. With supreme ill manners the new bypass road was made along its side, and across its front: demolition was threatened. But a saviour was at hand: a few years ago a distinguished London architect, Mr William Whitfield—himself a native of County Durham—bought the house. It is he who has restored it and given it an incomparable setting in the drastically reduced land that still remains with it. In the old wing there are several good panelled rooms: if this were all, St Helen would still be a house worthy of affection and preservation. But to move from the old wing to the new is to move from a modest manor house in north-east England into a grand palazzo on the banks of the Brenta. The *Garden Hall*, the *Library*, the *Dining Room* on the ground floor there—all fine rooms—lead on and up to the *Drawing Room* on the *piano nobile*. Here is a room of lofty proportions, with two great windows for the sun to pour through and from which to survey the garden. And beyond is the final revelation: the *Saloon*, a room of even greater size and even greater splendour, with a rococo ceiling of swags and masks and garlands, of birds and monkeys, and Cupid himself with his bow and arrows, a room with the perfection of a Palladian masterpiece. Three great windows here look down into the garden—a garden which might be a garden in Florence, an enclosed court of grass and flagstones, with monumental clipped hedges which already exclude all sight of factories and industrial litter. 'Remember' remarks the new owner, 'some of the finest palaces in Venice are in the tattiest surroundings.' But in the garden here there is little hint of the outside world—or of the 'O.K. Bus Services' swishing past on the busy road outside. To the north stand the former *stables* (now converted into a separate house)—all that remains of what was once a spreading wing of the Hall, built in a rather earlier Vanbrugian style, a handsome building with arched and rusticated windows. To the west of this group is the *church*, with its low, rugged, almost fortified exterior—a bellcote at the west end,. and imposing two-storeyed, battlemented porch. Much of the building is of late Norman or Transitional date; the interior has solid, simple arcades, an ancient roof on a Perpendicular clerestory, and an Early English chancel. The 'Cosin' pews shewn in an old engraving have, alas, been swept away, but there are stalls of this date in the choir, a couple of small brasses (1450 and 1558), and several Eden hatchments. The long broad street.of grim blackened terrace houses leads on to the west, to West Auckland.

Auckland, West [10] A long village of wide greens bordered by a string of blackened stone cottages and taller houses, with the traffic of the A68 and the A688 swirling through; the colliery is no more, but there are minor factories, and the

St Andrew Auckland or South Church, **Bishop Auckland**, and a detail of the Anglo-Saxon cross therein

St Helen Hall, **St Helen Auckland**: the Saloon

air of 19th-century industry hangs
heavy upon it. There has been some
attempt at smartening the place up
in recent years, and some rebuilding of houses along the green. On

the south side is a long 17th-
century house, with mullioned
windows and central porch
crowned with a decorative gable.
On the other side of the green,

half-screened by lime trees, stands
West Auckland Hall, the ancient
seat of the Eden family. Robert
Eden, eldest son of John Eden of
Bellasis and Windlestone (*see* Kirk

Vermiculation on the Palladian façade of St Helen Hall (*see also p. 35*)

Merrington), who was born in 1548, acquired West Auckland by marriage with the heiress of the Hutton family. The earliest part of the house, built on an H-plan, with twin gables, and low squat tower rising behind the centre of this south front, must date back to his time. It was his great-grandson, another John, who after the Civil War transformed the house in late 17th-century taste: a front door with segmental pediment and sash windows adorn the front. A late 17th-century panelled room, subsequently moved to Windlestone, is now in the Bowes Museum at Barnard Castle. When Windlestone became the chief Eden seat West Auckland sank in status, and for a time was used as a brewery. It now stands faded, beautiful and sad as a reminder of a great Durham family now, alas, departed from its ancestral county. Sir Robert Eden, son of Colonel John Eden the Royalist (whose father had raised a regiment of foot for Charles I), was created a baronet by Charles II in

1672. Since then, in the past three hundred years, the family has obtained a second baronetcy, two baronies and two earldoms; has produced a Governor-General of India, and the last English Governor of Maryland, seven Members of Parliament, two English Diocesan Bishops and one Primus of the Scottish Church, three Generals and an Admiral, two Cabinet Ministers and a Prime Minister and K.G. Sir William Eden, 7th Bt, was a gifted painter, and Sir Timothy Eden, 8th Bt, an accomplished author, who has given us the best book on County Durham to be published in recent years—the two volumes of *Durham* in the County Book series (Robert Hale, 1952). Sir John Eden, 9th Bt, is a Privy Councillor and former Minister. In all, this must seem quite a remarkable galaxy of talent from one family from West Auckland. The *Eden Arms*, near their erstwhile home, and (rather oddly) the Eden Bus Services, keep their name alive here in Auckland.

Aycliffe [16] The parent, as it were, of the new town of Newton Aycliffe (q.v.), but a village still, albeit cut in half by the old Great North Road (A167). The new A1 motorway roars by to the east, and the main railway line from King's Cross to Edinburgh runs in between. Imposing *church* with tall tower, incorporating Saxon work, but now chiefly of the 12th and 13th centuries. Spacious interior with 'engaged' aisles and a wealth of 17th-century pews. Many Saxon fragments. (*See also* Newton Aycliffe.)

Barnard Castle [15] An ancient, venerable and indeed charming market town on the banks of the River Tees: wide streets, lined with handsome 18th-century stone houses, lead to the market place, presided over by the 18th-century market cross or town hall, and, lying a little way back, the mediaeval parish church. To travellers coming from all directions except the south there is no

West Auckland Hall

Blagroves House, **Barnard Castle** ▷

sign of any castle; but the castle is there all right, presiding over the bridge and the rocky banks of the river. So this is undoubtedly the place from which to start a tour of the town. Barnard Castle takes its name from Bernard, son of Guy Balliol, who was granted land here by William II in 1093; soon after, Bernard began to build a castle on the rugged escarpment here to defend the north bank of the river. Above the bridge (which dates from 1569) on the rocky hillside, stands *Northam Tower*, and below this steep steps ascend to the *castle*. From this path there is a thrilling view of the river below, and the castle is entered by the North Gate. *The Round Tower* (or Balliol Tower) stands at the north-west corner of the inner court, rebuilt in the early 14th century on its Norman foundations (there is a low vaulted undercroft of this date); to the south are the remains of the 15th-century *Great Chamber* (with oriel window), and of the Great Hall. The lower parts of the Northam Tower are 13th century—the

The Market Cross at **Barnard Castle**

upper parts collapsed in the 19th—and there are fragments of other towers on the north side of the Inner Ward. After the attainder of the Balliols Barnard Castle was granted by the Crown to Guy Beauchamp, Earl of Warwick; thence through Warwick the King-Maker it passed to his daughter, the wife of Richard III—whose emblem, the boar, is to

be seen on the wall of the Great Chamber. Sir George Bowes of Streatlam garrisoned the castle for Elizabeth I in the 1569 Rebellion; but in 1626 Sir Henry Vane bought the place from the Crown, and his grandson took its name for the title of his barony in 1698. It remained in the hands of his descendants until 1952, when the 10th Lord Barnard presented it to the Minis-

try of Works. It is now beautifully maintained by the Department of the Environment, and green lawns and neat paths divide the Town Ward from the Middle Ward, and the Middle Ward from the Inner Ward, and it is possible from the surviving walls to gain some idea of the original extent of the castle. Returning to the river, *Bridgegate* leads up to *Thorngate* (right), a

Barnard Castle

street of 18th-century town houses which descends to a footbridge over the river, and old mill buildings, and (left) into *The Bank*, the street that leads up to the *Market Cross*. On the right is *Blagroves House*, a 16th-century house with a gabled bay window three storeys high. Here and in the *Market Place* are more good 18th-century houses, and one or two old shop fronts. The *Market Cross* was built in 1747 and stands in the middle of the street: crowned by a cupola, this delightful octagonal building comprises an open Tuscan colonnade on the ground floor and the Town Hall above lit by Venetian windows in four of its eight sides. East of the

cross stands the *parish church*. The tower is a successful Perpendicular rebuilding of 1874: inside, the base of the tower is crowded with 18th- and 19th-century monuments. The north arcade of the nave is late Norman, the south 13th century; steps lead up to the chancel, which is in origin Norman, but the chancel arch and nave clerestory are Perpendicular. The whole church was much restored in the 19th century. In the north transept is the 14th-century tomb of Robert de Mortham, priest. The *Market Place* becomes *Horsemarket*; on the left is the *King's Head*, where Charles Dickens stayed, collecting his material for *Nicholas Nickleby*; the

street curves gently, lined with dignified 18th-century (and earlier) houses. At the far end the *Methodist church* (1894) with its imposing spire faces up *Gallgate*, another wide street of handsome stone houses. But now it is time to retrace our steps to the *Market Cross*, and walk (or drive) half a mile up *Newgate*. Here stands one of the most astonishing buildings in all England: the *Bowes Museum*. What might be some grand *Hotel de Ville* gracing a large square in a French town here stands overlooking a leafy road in a remote market town of northern England, gazing across to the hills and moorlands of County Durham and the North

special interest is the series of notable rooms from a number of English houses: a 17th-century room from West Auckland Hall; a portion of the early 18th-century gallery from Gilling Castle; a rococo Drawing Room from Chesterfield House, Mayfair; and a Victorian Gothic room from a house in Cheltenham. Indeed the spirit of fantasy pervades the whole collection: it is one of the great museums of England. It would be difficult for any building to stand close to, let alone stand up to, this incredible pile. Nevertheless, *Barnard Castle School* (1886) next door, with its restrained long Jacobean front crowned by a tall white cupola (by Clark and Mossop of Darlington; the chapel, 1910 by W. D. Caroe), makes a good job of it. And on the other side, nearer the town, in the shadow of the museum stands the *R.C. church*, where in the churchyard, behind the sanctuary, George Bowes and the Countess of Montalbo lie buried.

Barningham [15] A quiet lane from Greta Bridge makes its way south and reaches Barningham. A long wide green, stone cottages and larger houses, a church with a square tower, the Milbank Arms, the gates to Barningham Park and woodlands crowning the hillside to the south—that is all there is of Barningham, but it is perfect. The *church* was built in 1816, but Pritchett remodelled it in 1891, filling the early Gothic revival box with arcades and narrow aisles, and forming a chancel. There are a few Victorian memorials to Milbanks—most of whose monuments are at Well, in the North Riding. Beautiful churchyard with stone walls, old tombstones and formal yews. 18th-century gate piers lead up to *Barningham Park*, seat of the

Riding. The Bowes Museum is indeed French: it was built by a French architect, Jules Pellechet, working for an illegitimate Anglo-Scottish aristocrat and his French wife. George Bowes was the bastard son of the 10th Earl of Strathmore: from his father he inherited the vast Durham estates that had descended to him from his mother, and he married the French actress Josephine Benoite, Countess of Montalbo. Here, close to Streatlam (q.v.), they founded and endowed this immense museum, to be filled with their collection of continental *objets d'art*. The foundation stone was laid in 1869, but George Bowes and his wife both died before the

museum was opened in 1892. Financial difficulties dogged the museum in later years, but in 1952 the Durham County Council took over its administration, and it is now admirably run, and has over the years received great additions to its original collections. There is no space here to describe these in detail: there are excellent guide books available. Suffice to say that there are rooms devoted to local antiquities from Roman times to the 19th century; great galleries of French furniture and china, and of Spanish and Italian pictures (including two Goyas and two Canalettos); there is also important needlework and silver. Perhaps of

The Causey Arch (*see* **Beamish**), 'the oldest railway bridge in the world'

'The Shepherd and Shepherdess', **Beamish**

Milbanks, baronets. A late 18th-century stable block stands close to the gates: the drive leads on and up to the house, with its attendant wings and appendages and garden walls. A late 17th-century house, the main front faces east: a rusticated front door with segmental pediment, and three storeys of sash windows—it is a dignified, simple composition. The ground rises sharply to the south: steps lead down from the first floor drawing room on this front, on to the terraced garden. 'Hanging' gardens with woodland walks, bright with azaleas in spring, descend to the more formal terraces. The Milbanks, a younger branch of the Milbankes of Halnaby (*see* Washington and Seaham), first came to Barningham in the mid-17th century.

Beamish [4] An unexpected rural hamlet, only a short way off the built-up road from Stanley to Chester-le-Street (A693): a jolly Georgian public house, *The Shepherd and Shepherdess*, with splendid lead figures over the porch, and a large clock face in the wing to the right. And so to *Beamish Hall*, standing in its undulating park not far from the lane. The estate belonged to the Wrays in the 16th century (*see* Tanfield), who, as Royalists, lost it in the Civil War. After the Restoration it was acquired by the Davisons, Newcastle merchants, and passed by marriage to a junior branch of the Eden family (*see* West Auckland), and again by marriage to the Shaftos (*see* Whitworth). The east part of the south front is a tall five-bay stone house of 1737: great late 19th- and early 20th-century additions were made to the west and north. In 1970 the place was acquired for the Beamish Museum. The *Beamish Open Air Museum* is unique in England: in the park on the opposite side of the lane there is being constructed (or reconstructed) a remarkable collection of industrial relics of workaday north-east England. The old Rowley station (from Rowley near Consett) serves a railway line plied by an old North Eastern Railway 'C' class locomotive (built in Gateshead in 1889) which hauls a train on which passengers can be carried—at present only a short distance, but in time the line will be much extended. An old Gateshead tram of 1925 carries visitors through a Northern Industrial Town (at present under construction) to other sights. A Victorian colliery is being recreated; there is a transport collection—with more old trams, and buses, and steam engines, and horse-drawn vehicles, and motor cars; the home farm is being restored to its former glory; and there are many period exhibits in Beamish Hall itself, together

63

with a restaurant and 'Edwardian' bar. The remaining part of the house is used as a teacher training college. Two miles to the north-west (continue up the lane beyond the house, and turn right at the T-junction) is an older relic, in its original site—the *Causey Arch*. Built in 1727 by Ralph Wood, it is a single-span stone arch across a deep ravine, designed to carry horse-drawn coal wagons from a local colliery. It is at present being restored (as part of Beamish Museum) and may claim to be the oldest railway bridge in the world.

Bearpark [10] Nothing to do with bears: the name is a corruption of *beau repaire*, the country retreat of the mediaeval priors of Durham. A few crumbling remains of their house survive in the valley to the north-east but very little of the handsome fragments illustrated by Robert Billings in his *Architectural Antiquities of the County of Durham* (1846). Bearpark is now a Victorian colliery village on the minor hilltop road from Durham to Lanchester: the pit in the background, terraces of miners' cottages, and an attractive little *church* by Hodgson Fowler (1879), with bellcote and lancet windows. Beautifully decorated interior: a lofty nave leads to a chancel adorned with lancets and blind arcades. The road leads on to Ushaw College, Esh and Quebec, with panoramic views over moorlands with, here and there, an industrial village in the valley below.

Belmont [10] Just out of Durham on the main road to Sunderland: a long street of stone, stucco and brick. At a fork in the road the *church* (1857) by Butterfield—his only building in the county. It is small, and without aisles or tower, but with its wide roof and porch with cat-slide roof displays some Butterfieldian character. *Belmont Hall* (now usually known as Ramside Hall) is now an hotel; it was the home of the Pembertons of Haw-

thorn Tower (q.v.). It is of stucco, battlemented, with castellated angle turrets—an informal, playful early 19th-century exterior. There is little of architectural interest within: the emphasis is on bars and fitted carpets.

Billingham [17] is an ancient place. The tower of the *parish church*—which unexpectedly looks across open fields on one side—is Saxon (10th century); the nave is perhaps even earlier, though here 12th-century arcades have been inserted. In 1939 a new chancel with wider aisles was added (by G. E. Charlewood), an effective late Gothic addition, to provide for the needs of the great population of the new I.C.I. town, which has sprung up along the banks of the Tees. There is still the faint air of an overgrown village round the church. But not far away is the great new town round the *Billingham Centre* (turn right, off A19, going north). Here is a large pedestrian shopping precinct, the Billingham Forum—with a first-rate theatre, an art gallery, and a skating rink—a tall circular block of flats looking like a great brick gasometer, and, in the middle of all this, the Billingham Arms in neo-neo-Georgian, with sash windows and urns in this forest of concrete and glass. But take the road to Haverton Hill (east at the roundabout near the parish church) and drive along the road through the I.C.I. works. This is one of the most extraordinary of experiences, a sight almost unique in England. On either side of the road are the works, steaming, sizzling—tall steel chimneys, great cylinders, pipes everywhere. The road goes on and on, to Haverton Hill and Port Clarence (q.v.): there are acres and acres of this remarkable landscape. And from the distance, too, this landscape is remarkable. Take the A19 at dusk from Easington to Peterlee: from the high ground here is the vast panorama, with lights

twinkling, the smoke and the vapours rising, illuminated too, perhaps, by the setting sun. Or from the south, from the foothills of the Cleveland Hills behind Middlesbrough, from a bedroom window at Ormesby Hall at night, the whole industrial world along the banks of the Tees comes to life in an extraordinary way, brilliant with a thousand lights, the great girders of the Transporter Bridge dark in silhouette: a magic city.

Binchester [10] The name brings echoes of a hymn tune ('Happy are they, they that love God') composed by Dr Croft—but apparently not so named by him: Dr Croft was, after all, of Herefordshire, not of County Durham. *Binchester Blocks* is a grey, drab village, on the lane to Byers Green. The site of the *Roman fort* (Vinovium) is due north of Bishop Auckland, close to the river. A hypocaust survives, but there is little else to see; some of the large blocks of stone were reused at Escomb church (q.v.). Binchester Hall, a modest early 19th-century house, is now an hotel. Good views of Auckland Castle from the lane that hugs the river here.

Birtley [4] Great industrial sprawl between Gateshead and Chester-le-Street; the new dual carriageway of the A1 (M) bypasses the place on the higher ground to the east; the old Great North Road (now A6127) passes modern factories and housing estates to the west. What remains of the old village lies in between. At the crossroads here is the *monument to Colonel Moseley Perkins*, a white marble figure of 1874—a really rather amusing affair. Colonel Perkins lived at Birtley Hall, and was a local colliery owner who interested himself in the welfare of his miners and was an enthusiastic promoter of the local Volunteer battalion; he was also a Parliamentary candidate—but died suddenly. His family gave their name to Perkinsville (*see*

Pelton). The *church* stands a little further south, a Norman revival building of 1848 by Pickering, who rebuilt St Mary-the-Less, Durham, in the same style, with west tower, apsidal sanctuary, and other embellishments. Open ground nearby, with wide prospects of council estates and schools—and factories in the valley below, which stretch along the old main road as far as Pelaw.

Bishop Auckland *see* Auckland, Bishop

Bishop Middleham [10] 'Bishop' Middleham because there was in the middle ages a castle here belonging to the Bishop of Durham: there is no vestige of it remaining. The village lies between the A1 motorway and the A177 (Durham to Stockton): to approach the place from the north is disappointing, because the street is lined with glum Victorian industrial cottages. But at the bottom the old village is intact: the *Hall* is an 18th-century house, probably the refacing of an earlier building. The *church* is raised above the street and outwardly is unremarkable, with a mere bell turret. Inside it is spacious: wide nave and aisles of the early 13th-century; font of Frosterley marble; two early hatchments—one of 1680 to the widow of Thomas Bedford, a former incumbent, the other to a Hutton of Mainsforth. But the most interesting thing in the church is the monument to Robert Surtees, the renowned historian of County Durham (1779–1834), who lived at Mainsforth Hall in this parish. Near it is another tablet to General Sir Herbert Conyers Surtees (1858–1933), himself a considerable local antiquary. *Mainsforth* is a mile to the west; the Hall, home of the Surtees, stood four square, a handsome early 18th-century mansion, three storeys high, with hipped roof, generous quoins and sturdy chimneys. Overcome by

proximity to Ferryhill, and coal, it was demolished in 1962. The high garden walls survive, punctuated by gate piers crowned with urns. Peering through the iron gates now the eye meets the sight of an incongruous suburban villa. 'And so farewell to you, Robert Surtees, and farewell to Mainsforth' wrote Sir Timothy Eden, 'farewell to that sweet retreat amongst the trees and peacocks, dear to me for your sake, and dear for later ties; where I, too, have dined and talked with one bearing your name, and skilled, as you, in ancient lore, and hospitable and kind as you were—and watched the evening sun slant through the window painted with your famous ermine coat' (*Durham*, vol. 2, Robert Hale, 1952).

Bishopton [17] A meeting place of minor roads in the unspoiled countryside north-west of Stockton. The *church* stands above the village street: it incorporates fragments from the mediaeval building, but was mostly rebuilt in 1846 by Sharpe and Paley. An inscription on the west wall commemorates Thomas Holgate, for twenty-eight years vicar of the parish, and his three sisters, 'who at their sole cost out of a slender income rebuilt this church and gave the bells, the clock, the books and the silver plate for Holy Communion'. There is too much light fumed oak and grained woodwork, but with its little Victorian reredos and 19th-century glass it delightfully reflects the piety of the period. *Castle Hill* to the south is an early British earthwork.

Blackhall [11] A blackened stretch of coast—as black as its prophetic name implies. The line of the coast, the line of the railway from Sunderland to Hartlepool, the line of the main road (A1086)—all run parallel to each other within a narrow half mile. The Blackhall Colliery, one of the great collieries of the Durham coast, and—a little further north—the Horden Col-

liery, make this a grimy industrialized stretch of country. In the hinterland is the great New Town of Peterlee. Grim terraces of miners' cottages, a public house or two, a church up a back street, a shabby alley leading across railway sidings to allotment gardens and the sea—such is Blackhall. To the south a path leads to Black Halls rocks, steep rocky coves, wild but polluted. To the north the Castle Eden burn, leaving its wooded dene, enters the sea. Half a mile inland along the road to Castle Eden stands *Hardwick Hall*, from the late 16th century till the early 19th the home of the recusant family of Maire (*see* Hutton Henry and Lartington). The south front is a modest 18th-century façade of two storeys, with parapet and giant angle pilasters—which conceals a much older rambling house behind. In 1590 Robert Maire was reconverted to the Roman faith; the intricate Priest's Hole survives, and is perhaps the work of that ingenious man, Father Richard Holtby, S.J. Hardwick passed into other hands in 1825—and the old Papist Mission moved to Hutton Henry.

Blaydon [4] Old industrial country along the south bank of the Tyne: Dunston, Swalwell, Blaydon, Stella—the housing and factories are continuous. In the early 18th century that great industrialist and ironmaster, Sir Ambrose Crowley of Mitcham, Surrey, established his ironworks at Swalwell—where he made everything from pins to anchors; his handsome monument stands in Mitcham church, with medallion portraits of himself (d. 1713) and his wife (d. 1727), close to Mitcham Grove—a far cry from the banks of the Tyne. The old Blaydon Racecourse was close to the junction of the Tyne and the Derwent; the races (immortalized in the old song) were last held in 1916, and the power station stands on the site.

Axwell Park (*see* **Blaydon**)

Axwell Park stands four-square against a wooded hillside, facing north across the Tyne. It is the finest 18th-century house in the county, and was built in 1758 by James Paine for Sir Thomas Clavering, 6th Baronet, of a family which had been established here since the 16th century, and received a baronetcy in 1661 in recognition of services to Charles I and Charles II. They became immensely rich from their collieries during the 18th century. The house stands in a splendid position, and Paine made full use of it. Of three storeys, in stone, with heavily rusticated ground floor, and central pediment, it is characteristic of Paine at his most grandiloquent. It is illustrated in Paine's *Plans, Elevations and Sections of Noblemen and Gentlemen's Houses* (1767); but now the Claverings are extinct and gone, and the house has become an industrial school, much of the park has been built over, and from the balustraded terrace there is now a view across industrial Tyneside, with coking works and smoking chimneys at its gates. The *Dower House* still stands, close to the main road, a pretty house with Georgian Gothick crenellations, and Gothick bays and Venetian windows, built about 1770. It is some consolation that both these houses survive—though in a somewhat beleaguered situation.

Boldon, East [5] A long street—with one good 18th-century brick house—on its low hill commanding wide views across the flat, featureless, built-up wastes towards Jarrow and South Shields. At the east end of the street stands the *church*, a red-brick basilica of 1922—with extensive additions of 1933: an effective building.

Boldon, West [5] A prominent landmark in the flat industrialized landscape south of Jarrow—for the low hill of Boldon is crowned by the 13th-century spire of the parish church: terraces of cottages surround it, and green fields divide the village from Jarrow and South Shields to the north, and from Sunderland and Washington to the south-east and south-west. There are wide views from the churchyard towards the cranes and shipyards of the Tyne. Important mediaeval *church* with unusual stumpy broach spire of the mid-13th century: intimate, well-furnished interior. The Boldon Book was the survey of the estates of the Bishopric of Durham made in 1183 by command of Bishop Pudsey: it is called the Boldon Book because so many entries are enumerated for the different properties, whose tenants and villeins are to 'hold, work and render as those of Boldon', the estate of Boldon being the first demesne in which details of such service are listed. *Boldon Hall* is a good medium-sized stone manor house of 1709, built by William Fawcett, whose arms adorn the pedimented front door. To the west stands, close to the dual carriageway, *Scot's House*, a somewhat grander building of 1798, with pedimented façade, earlier 18th-century wings and stables, and a Victorian Tudor gatehouse on the main road.

Bowburn [10] A sudden suburban eruption on the road from Durham to Stockton (A177): council houses, a factory or so, the Bowburn Hall Hotel, and a 1960s church—looking like a spaceship.

Bowes [14] Wild, inhospitable, magnificent country, with the Roman road (A66) charging through the long village street of gaunt stone houses and cottages, one standing back from the road being the original Dotheboys Hall of *Nicholas Nickleby*. At the west end of the village stands the Norman *castle keep*, a great square cliff of stone, defended now only by a trim grassy moat; indeed there are no signs of surrounding walls or buildings. From the great gaping windows are sweeping views across the North Riding. The castle was built for Henry II towards the end of the 12th century. The *church* nearby, modest outside with its bellcote and Victorian ventilator, is of considerable interest within. Long nave and chancel; low transepts. In the north transept is a large Roman slab with long inscription 'in honour of Emperors and Caesar ... by the first cohort of the Thracian cavalry' (c. 204), and near the north door are two fonts, one 12th century, one mounted on a Roman altar. In the sanctuary a tablet commemorates Cornelius Harrison of Stubb House 'Patron of this church' (1806) (*see* Winston); another in the nave Thomas Emerson Headlam, M.P. and Privy Councillor (1861). The most beautiful feature is the mediaeval carved stone Crucifixion outside the south porch, which has miraculously survived. Church and castle stand at the north-east corner of the Roman fort of Lavatrae, of which only a few ditches are visible. North of the crossroads is the derelict railway station—a charming building—on the old line to Barnard Castle.

Brancepeth [10] South-west of Durham, beyond the shabby growth of Brandon, there is open

West Boldon church

country for a few miles before the A690 reaches Willington. In this oasis is Brancepeth. At the crossroads are tidy terraces of estate cottages; and the road south leads to the castle and the church. At first sight the *castle* looks tremendous: across the broad grass sward round towers like fat chessmen mark the entrance gateway, and behind the forbidding walls battlemented towers look down. On closer inspection it is only too obvious that much of what we see is 19th-century work, and 19th-century work at its most grandiloquent. Some of the detail is crude, but the grand effect is undoubtedly terrific.

Brancepeth was originally held by the Bulmer family, passed from them by marriage in the 13th century to the Nevilles, Earls of Westmorland, who forfeited it to the Crown after the 1569 rebellion. Sold by the Crown, it passed through various hands until purchased by William Russell, banker and coal owner of Sunderland, in 1796. It was his son Matthew who employed an Edinburgh architect, John Patterson, to restore and enlarge the castle in 1837. Matthew Russell married Tennyson's aunt: it was his brother-in-law, Charles Tennyson-d'Eyncourt, who built the equally fantastic Bayons

67

Brancepeth church (*see also p. 27*)

Manor in Lincolnshire, and the two men shared the same tastes. It was Charles Tennyson-d'Eyncourt who acted as arbiter of taste, and assisted his brother-in-law in collecting armour and works of art for Brancepeth. Creevy notes that Matthew Russell spent £80,000 a year for several years at Brancepeth. The castle, as revived, contained a Baron's Hall, an Armour Gallery and a private chapel—as well as other useful amenities such as a Billiard Room, a Library and a Smoking Room, all of great size. Portions of the old castle of the Nevilles survive in basements and bastions and in some of the masonry. But most of the glorious skyline of towers and turrets and battlements—specially effective when seen from the south—is the re-creation of Matthew Russell. Tennyson wrote:

'Far and near / From every side come noisy swarms / Of peasants in their homely gear, / And mixed with these to Brancepeth came / Grave gentry of estate and name, / And captains known for worth in arms.'

Brancepeth subsequently descended to Russell's son-in-law, the 7th Viscount Boyne (the Hamilton-Russell family); in this century it became for a time the headquarters of the Durham Light Infantry, but it is at present unused and alarming notices warn visitors of the presence of Securicor guard dogs. Across the grass stands the *church* with its bold west tower and handsome grouping of clerestoried nave, north porch, transepts, north-east chapel and chancel. The lower stages of the tower are 12th century, the upper 13th, the crown

Perpendicular; the nave clerestory north-east chapel, and chancel are Perpendicular also. The porch is a distinguished 17th-century addition, a delightful amalgam of Classical and Gothic, with pilasters and cherubs' heads, but Gothic doorways, the work of Bishop Cosin who became rector of Brancepeth in 1626 and Bishop of Durham in 1660. His porch is an introduction to the glorious interior, furnished by him in the years before the Civil War. The nave arcades are Early English; the clerestory is Perpendicular. There are Decorated windows in aisles and transepts. Here there is a great array of pews (with grand family pews in the transepts), two-decker pulpit with elaborate pinnacled tester, and font cover. The sumptuous screen with its canopied entrance and return stalls leads into the chancel

Brancepeth Castle (*see also p. 33*) ▷

At **Brignall**

resplendent with arcaded stalls and panelling, altar and altar rails. The ceiling, too, with its carved pendants is Cosin's. The carver was one Robert Barker, and the re-furnishing began in 1638. Cosin's Gothic Revival, to be found also at the Cathedral, at Sedgefield, in the chapel of Auckland Castle, and elsewhere, is unique to County Durham. It is a conscious attempt to refurbish the churches of the Bishoprick, despoiled by the Reformation or Civil War, in the fashion of the mediaeval ideal. It

was a noble achievement, and the happy juxtaposition of Gothic and Classical details is delightful. Above the chancel arch, on the nave side, are mysterious frag-ments of (perhaps) an earlier rood screen. There are also in the church important Neville tombs: the stone effigy of Robert Neville (1319), the wooden effigy of Ralph, 2nd Earl of Westmorland and his wife, and the stone tomb-chest of Ralph, 3rd Earl. There are also two small brasses, one to Thomas Claxton (1403), the other to Richard Drax,

a priest (1456). The road north from the crossroads leads to *Quarry Hill*, a tall, three-storied, gabled, symmetrical house of the early 17th century.

Brandon [10] The A690 (Durham to Crook) rattles through the drab main street of this large colliery vil-lage: other drab streets turn off to right and left. Handsome late Vic-torian *church*—with rather more architectural detail and style than the run-of-the-mill erections in so many colliery villages. And there is

70

an attractive little *R. C. church*, further down the road.

Brignall [15] The romantic ruin of the *ancient church* lies close to the River Greta: the narrow lane from Greta Bridge climbs slowly, with many twists and turns, to the *new church* (1833 by R. Dawson) close to the village. It has a tall tower with long lancet windows, and is a simple gothic revival box. Splendid views north from the churchyard, to the lands beyond the Tees. Farms and cottages in enclosed gardens across the meadows. An adorable spot.

Burnmoor [4] (Bournmoor) The Victorian *church* of yellow brick, patterned and diapered with red, stands opposite the Victorian south entrance to Lambton Park: gates and lodge, church and vicarage, all as it were to match. The church was erected by the 2nd Earl of Durham in 1867, and the chancel and sanctuary were richly decorated by Johnson and Hicks in 1881. But the remarkable thing is the enormous marble figure of Nike—a winged Victory—standing in the north aisle, erected by the 5th Earl in memory of his father and uncle in 1929. It is the work of Waldo Storey, R.A. (Rome, 1894). Lambton tombs in churchyard, and a prospect to the south of angry chimneys and council houses—and more distant hills beyond.

Burnopfield [4] Up the hill from Gibside; roads to Whickham and Gateshead, to Consett and Stanley; a Victorian *church* (1872) with gabled east end, bellcoted west end; a few larger houses, and the usual terraces of 19th-century cottages.

Byers Green [10] Visiting this somewhat plain village, down a meandering lane off the main road from Spennymoor to Bishop Auckland, and close to the River Wear, it is not easy to imagine Thomas Wright, astronomer, architect and

The **Castle Eden** brewery

landscape gardener living here in the 18th century. It was here that he built his retreat, laid out his terraces and wooded walks, and planted his groves; from here he could enjoy the prospect of the surrounding countryside, the river and Durham Cathedral. He conceived it all as a Tuscan villa, imagining himself as Pliny, entertaining his friends and poring over his books, manuscripts and drawings. All this, 19th-century industrialism obliterated; and Thomas Wright, architect of Nuthall Temple and the wings at Shugborough, landscape gardener at Badminton, astronomer and mathematician, is forgotten or unknown. There is a plain Victorian Gothic *church* at the entrance to the village. (*See also* Westerton.)

Castle Eden [11] An oasis between Peterlee and Hartlepool: a road to the coast turns off the dual carriageway of the A19, and leads to the village. The park lies below on the left: on the right stands the Castle Eden *Brewery*, a charming little whitewashed group, with a cupola crowning the central pediment, originally built in the late 18th century as a cotton mill. A lane leads off to the church and the park gate—the *church* a delightful amalgam of Classical and Gothick. 'This sacred edifice', reads the inscription over the vestry door, 'which consuming time had now reduced to ruinous decay was rebuilt by Rowland Burdon in 1764.' Lead-covered spire; stately little nave with Corinthian columns painted blue, the capitals gilded,

71

Gothick windows and a Gothick Venetian east window; elaborate oak screen in the style of the 17th century; 18th-century oval marble font. A tablet in the chancel commemorates Rowland Burdon, M.P. for County Durham 1790–1805, who designed and built the first iron bridge at Sunderland, 'a performance alike remarkable for originality of invention and for public spirit'. A window in the nave (by L. C. Evetts) commemorates another Rowland Burdon, 'sixth and last surviving of his name' who died in 1944. The *Hall*, built by the first Rowland Burdon, is a late 18th-century three-storeyed castellated house with sash windows and

central bay window, and a later Gothick palm house screening the ground floor; it was designed by William Newton of Newcastle. But the second Rowland Burdon met Sir John Soane, then a young and unknown architect, in Naples in 1778—and Soane accompanied Burdon and his friends to Mantua, Parma and Venice. Soane subsequently produced designs for Castle Eden and it is possible that its later Gothick dress is Soane's work: it has something in common with other Gothick work of his (e.g. at Port Eliot). After the death of the last Rowland Burdon it was used for a while as offices by the National Coal Board; it now belongs to the

Peterlee Corporation, and awaits restoration. The park is a golf course. *Castle Eden Dene*, to the north of the house, is the most extensive and most beautiful of all Durham denes, with the burn running deep between wooded banks to the sea. Here the second Rowland Burdon created a romantic garden, complete with caves and grottoes, and picturesque prospects and features. This is now being rescued and restored by the Peterlee Corporation, and is open to the public.

Chester-le-Street [4] From the terrace at Lumley Castle, Chester-le-Street looks an attractive

Bridge over the Wear, **Chester-le-Street**

town, with the formation of the hills, the great railway viaduct, the tall spire of the church, the huddle of houses. Especially is this so at evening, or at twilight, when details become blurred. In daylight, when driving—or walking—through its streets, the town is a disappointment. Raw red council houses line the outer roads: the main streets contain few buildings that call for any comment. Yet Chester, as its name suggests, was a Roman station—but of this there is nothing to be seen. The 'street' is, of course, the Great North Road, but the town is now bypassed by the A1 (M), which roars on its way to the east of Lumley Castle. To the west is the important railway line to Newcastle and Edinburgh. The *Church* is well worth a visit; indeed the spire (c. 1400) is the finest in the county, rising 189 feet from an octagon which in turn crowns a heavily buttressed Early English tower. The spire is 'engaged' by the south aisle; and on the north side by the curious *anchorage* or hermit's dwelling built here at the end of the 14th century. There are rooms within, with a squint opening into the church from which to watch the altar. Inside, the Early English nave of five bays is long and dark—the whole church filled with Victorian glass—and in the chancel are Early English sedilia, and piscina, of elegant and beautiful work. The Lumley Chapel (north side) was rebuilt by Bonomi in 1832. Along the wall of the north aisle is a line of mediaeval tombs—a row of fourteen formidable knights. These are the Lumleys, ancestors of Lord Scarbrough. Some are genuine, some mere impersonations of this ancient race, but all were brought together here at the end of the 16th century by John, 7th Lord Lumley. Some real Lumleys he brought from Durham Cathedral; to these he added some fictitious 'ancestors' from dissolved monasteries, and had others newly carved for the purpose—interest-

ing 16th-century fakes. To squeeze them all in, some of the older effigies had to have their feet chopped off, in Procrustean fashion: even so, they make a fine display. The series of family monuments is continued at Cheam in Surrey, and at Saxby St Helen in Lincolnshire. To the south of the town, in its own little park, stands the *Hermitage*, an early 19th-century stone Tudor house; and to the west is *Southill Hall*, a late-Georgian house, standing in its own well-wooded grounds; beyond, is an unexpected stretch of wilder country with bracken—and extensive views. *Lumley Castle* stands against its wooded hillside to the east, across the River

Wear. It was built c. 1390 by Sir Ralph Lumley, and is still the property of his descendant, the 12th Earl of Scarbrough, though used as an hotel. The building is quadrangular, with four square towers at the corners. A gatehouse on the east side leads into the central court: opposite, another gatehouse, crowned with an 18th-century cupola and clock, is the entrance to the Great Hall. John Lord Lumley decorated both gatehouses with a string of heraldic shields, and the Hall with a great chimneypiece, a set of specially painted ancestral portraits, and an equestrian statue of his legendary Saxon ancestor, Liulph, founder

Deerhouse, **Coatham Mundeville**

of the line. It was here that Lord Lumley entertained James I. The king, exasperated by the Bishop of Durham's fulsome account of their host's distinguished ancestry, stopped the Bishop. 'I didna ken' he said, 'that Adam's name was Lumley.' In 1721 Vanbrugh refashioned the castle for the 2nd Earl of Scarbrough: its rugged, mediaeval mien he retained—but he enlarged the *Great Hall*, and on the west front raised a wide terrace, with a new doorway to the hall; the cupola was added, and sash windows, with a row of oval lights above, replaced the mediaeval, and orderly rows of sashes appeared elsewhere. Inside, the *Undercroft* (now the hotel Dining Room) on the south front is a room of great distinction, vaulted, with boldly rusticated pillars upholding the ceiling—an echo of his undercroft at Grimsthorpe. On the first floor of the south-west tower he formed a great *ballroom*, known as the Garter Room, where Francesco Vassali decorated the walls and coved ceiling with superb plasterwork (c.

1730), introducing the motif of the garter in celebration of the Earl's K.G. The 3rd Earl inherited the great estates of the Earls of Castleton in Yorkshire and Lincolnshire; thereafter Sandbeck became the chief family seat—and Lumley was left to slumber, only occasionally occupied as a family home. For a time it was used by Durham University; now, as has been said, it is an hotel. The castle looks magnificent—from any angle; and within there are delightful rooms—on the first floor, for instance, where some contain 18th-century decoration, others retain earlier panelling and features. From the windows there are wide views, across the park and River Wear, or, within, into the secluded grassed and paved garden in the courtyard below.

Chilton [10] The traveller on the old North Road, encountering in pleasant countryside this sudden apparition—suburban terraces, shops, a school, a 1920s church, all in hard red brick—might well ask

'Why?' It is, of course, one of those villages that grew up overnight to serve a local colliery, a colliery now dead. But those hard red Victorian terraces go on. Vintage Durham.

Chopwell [3] A sprawling colliery village north of the Derwent with terrace after terrace, row after row, of council houses and older cottages, the *church* outside the village on the edge of moorland, in a somewhat watered-down Gothic of 1906: an interior of well-polished woodwork and tinted glass.

Church Kelloe *see* Kelloe

Cleadon [5] Between South Shields and Sunderland, and inland from the coast, the old village is an unexpected oasis; little Victorian stone *church* with apse and white-painted bellcote, a village pond, and one or two old cottages. *Cleadon House* is a good-looking red-brick house of 1738 with Venetian window facing the village street; nearby stands *Cleadon Tower*, a small Tudor house built

Consett

round a square (perhaps earlier) tower in its north-west angle.

Coatham Mundeville [16]

On one side the main railway line to Edinburgh: on the other the old Great North Road. Now on the third the A1 motorway, with an interchange roundabout, has arrived; yet Coatham survives as a village, and is indeed but a handful of houses, and a small Victorian *church*, by R. J. Withers, 1865. The most interesting building is *Hall Garth*, outwardly an 18th-century L-shaped house, but inwardly much older. It stands in a little park, with an 18th-century stone *deerhouse*, and a large walled garden with spaces for stoves in the walls—to coerce the fruit trees or whatever else was grown thereon. The house is now an hotel, but was until recently home of the Summerson family: Sir John Summerson, Keeper of Sir John Soane's Museum and eminent art historian, is a member of this family, and a native of Darlington.

Cockfield [15]

The long village street climbs up to Holy Moor, the wide common which spreads across the hilltop, commanding wide views of industrial Weardale to the north, and the expanse of Hamsterley Forest to the west. The *church* is at the bottom of the street, and at first sight appears Victorian: in fact the south wall of the nave and chancel is 13th century, with narrow lancet windows: the chancel was extended to the east and the nave to the west, and the north aisle built, in 1911. The nave is panelled with 17th-century pew-backs, and in the chancel floor are two 14th-century memorials, one inscribed to Roger Vavasour, the other bearing the worn figure of a girl. In Cockfield was born in 1731 George Dixon, coal owner, geologist, chemist, mathematician, engraver and china painter, inventor of coal gas and colliery engineer. His great-uncle, the first George Dixon, was

steward at Raby in the 17th century; his portrait used to hang at the castle until it was presented to a descendant some years ago. His brother was Jeremiah Dixon, the astronomer, who was employed with Charles Mason to survey the boundaries of Pennsylvania and Maryland (the 'Mason-Dixon line'). The great-grandson of George Dixon II was John Dixon, engineer of London, who brought Cleopatra's Needle to England in 1878.

Coniscliffe, High [16]

A dramatic sight across the River Tees: the church with its spire, and the gabled Victorian rectory next door, stand perched on a rocky cliff above the river. And dramatic views can be obtained across the river and its level meadows from the churchyard. The church is Early English and of unusual length—accentuated by the absence of a south aisle; simple Early English arcade to the north aisle. The church was restored and re-roofed in 1846—indeed the engraving in Billings's *Architectural Antiquities of the County of Durham* (1845) shows the work in progress. 15th-century chancel stalls; 12th-century tomb slab in porch; late 17th-century monument to a Bowes (of Thornton Hall) in chancel. The village street is attractive with Georgian houses and cottages. And a mile or two to the north-east (lying back from the B6279) stands *Thornton Hall*. Tall and gabled, partly 16th century, partly 17th, with some 18th-century sash windows inserted in its south front, and with old farm buildings at its side, it looks across the road to an ancient avenue of trees in the meadow opposite.

Consett [3]

The sight of Consett is both terrible and magnificent: from far away—crossing the moors from Lanchester to Stanhope, or driving by the side of the Derwent Reservoir, or motoring south from Cor-

bridge on the A68, or in a sudden and unexpected view from Mugglesswick churchyard—Vulcan's great forges stand there on the hillside enveloped in steam: cooling towers, cylinders, chimneys, incredible and intimidating. Iron ore was discovered here in 1837: the works were first opened in 1840. The town itself is grimy and grim and of little interest: one or two wide streets of blackened Victorian shops with scarcely a single public building, a mean square with a flimsy clock—there is very little to see. The *parish church* is 1862 'Norman', with a stocky north-west tower (and a clock with Westminster chimes), and a wide, spacious attractively redecorated interior. The *R. C. church* nearby is a modern basilica: Byzantine arcades divide nave from aisles, and the sanctuary is lined in marble and mosaic. The grandest building in the middle of the town is the 1930s *Plaza Cinema*—magnifique! It is now the Marina Social and Bingo Club. The best way to see Consett is to turn off the A65 at Castle-side—where there is a pretty little *church* of 1863: an intimate devotional interior with apsidal sanctuary; and the *Smelter's Arms* opposite, with its appropriate and enormous inn sign—and make for Consett itself. Terraces of pre-war council houses lead on and up—and here the steelworks make their first full impact. A great viaduct (by Sir Thomas Bouch, 1856) carries the railway across the valley, and great cliffs of slag occupy the foreground: beyond and above are the towering cylinders and chimneys, hissing and steaming, enveloped in smoke. The town itself is dull and somewhat tame after all this. But turn left into the square, past churches and past the Plaza, and the road descends to Blackhill. At the bottom of the hill, near the public gardens, is *St Aidan's* (1854) with a broach spire and central flèche. And not far beyond is the *R. C. church of St Mary* (1865 by Oliver and Leeson), memorable for its tall tower with elaborate pinnacled stair turret, which gives it an almost Flemish silhouette. The interior with its narrow apsidal chancel and imposing reredos, 19th-century glass and many objects of piety is reverent and beautiful. In the south-west of the churchyard are the tombs of priests who have served the church—including Henry Gillow (1915) of the recusant Lancashire family of furniture makers. Opposite is the gay façade of an old cinema or music hall—now closed—with comic bulbous domes, and the road descends past *St Andrew's United Reform church*, with its prickly little spire, to Shotley Bridge (q.v.). Everywhere are blackened cottages, everywhere the brooding presence of the steelworks, and great cliffs of slag.

Cornforth [10] Between the A1 motorway and the main railway line: great cement works on the road up from Ferryhill, and row upon row of miners' cottages which served the former colliery. But in the middle of all this is an unexpected village green with older cottages and one larger Georgian house—and on the edge of a steep slope a little red-brick Victorian *church* of 1860, with bellcote over the chancel arch. Views across the motorway—with the traffic thundering by.

Cotherstone [15] Close to the south bank of the River Tees, an excellent village of stone cottages and one or two larger houses, with the road (B6277) twisting and turning and providing different views and vistas of its charms. There is the steep mound of the castle above the spot where the Balder joins the Tees, with a few fragments of broken masonry—and a *church* of 1881 (by C. Purdon Clarke) of unmistakable Victorian outline, with an interior of pitch pine pews, bare stone walls, and a loud ticking clock.

Coundon [10] Victorian village of the former colliery, near Bishop Auckland: the usual gloomy terraces, the usual red-brick church.

Cowpen Bewley [17, 11] seems almost like a phantom village, here in the marsh. It is a mile or so north of Haverton Hill (q.v.), with the great chemical works not far away, the atomic power station, the steelworks, and shipping in the Tees in the background, and Seal Sands beyond all that, at the mouth of the river. There is a wide green, with a few old cottages, old brick walls, and *Ivy House*, a 17th-century brick farmhouse, with blocked-up windows and fragments of 'mannerist' decoration.

Cowshill [8] Upper Weardale: the land of old lead mines and waterfalls and wild craggy countryside. Good *church* of 1915, in Art Nouveau Gothic. A few miles to the west in still wilder, craggier country, close to the frontiers of Northumberland and Cumberland, is Killhope. Here in majestic isolation stands the great *Killhope Wheel*, with a few relics of industrial buildings, on the edge of the bleak moor. The wheel is 40 feet high: rushing water from the hillside turned it, to power the machinery for crushing the ore. It was built in 1860, and has recently been restored to serve as an awesome object of veneration for industrial archaeologists, and others.

Coxhoe [10] Main road village on the A177: bleak terraces, a flashy modern *R. C. church* on one side of the road—and, surrounded by trees and half screened by houses on the other, the *parish church* by R. J. Withers (1862); stone-built and demure, the north side is stuccoed, awaiting a north aisle that was never built. Coxhoe, however, has the distinction of being the birthplace in 1806 of Elizabeth Barrett Browning. Her parents had rented Coxhoe Hall for a few years, waiting for their house at Hope End in Herefordshire to be built: they left Coxhoe in 1809, and Elizabeth Barrett married Robert Browning in 1846. Coxhoe Hall stood on the higher ground to the north of the village; the house was built in the early 18th century, altered by James Paine in 1749, and subsequently given a Strawberry Hill Gothick dress and battlements; there was good plasterwork within. Occupied by Italian prisoners during the war, and subsequently left derelict, all was swept away in the 1950s. Only the tablet in Kelloe church (q.v.) recalls Elizabeth Barrett Browning's birth here.

Craghead [4] Colliery village south of Stanley, on the spur of the hills with magnificent views to the east, towards Chester-le-Street and distant Penshaw. Built on the side of the hill is the *church* of 1912, an unremarkable affair, but most successfully redecorated by Mr Dykes-Bower in recent years.

Crimdon [11] Along the coast road south of Blackhall the Crimdon Beck, tumbling down from Hesleden enters the sea at Crimdon Dene: there are views along the coast to Hartlepool, and hopes of open sands. But at the *Sea Gull Inn* is the entrance to the Crimdon Caravan Camp: there are caravans, caravans, caravans—miles of them. Row upon row, road upon road, cars, caravans, campers.

Crook [9] The old collieries are extinct, and with the arrival of new industries the face of the town has been smartened up. A wide square with greens occupies the centre: on the east side is the *parish church*, a modest Victorian building of 1841 by Bonomi and Cory. On the higher ground behind stands the *R. C. church* of Our Lady Immaculate, a grand building of 1854 with commanding tower, by E. W. Pugin. The church was founded by three young Oxford converts, of

whom the most notable was Thomas William Wilkinson, afterwards Bishop of Hexham. There is glass by Atkinson, and a High Altar, brilliant with marble and mosaic, by Bentley. The road to the north leads up to Billy Row and Mount Pleasant, two now decayed colliery villages, euphemistically named in characteristic Durham manner.

Croxdale [10] Readers of the articles on Croxdale Hall in *Country Life* in September 1939 might be forgiven for imagining that Croxdale was in a remote and rural part of County Durham: in fact it is an incredible oasis, close to the Wear in between Spennymoor and Durham. Rows of miners' cottages line the main road through the village, and there is a small Victorian *church* built to serve the colliery village. But where the old A1 crosses the river there is a glimpse of a well-wooded park, a secret, mysterious place, inaccessible from the high bridge: this is Croxdale Hall. The Salvin family have owned it since the early 15th century, and still live here. They came into the place by marriage, having migrated from Thorpe Salvin, close to Sherwood Forest—their original name was le Silvan or 'of the woods'. *Croxdale Hall* is a stone house of c. 1760, with a seven-bay front with central Venetian window over a front door with Tuscan columns: the south front has a wide central pediment and faces the garden; the north front incorporates portions of the older house, and has wide bow windows; at the back long wings embrace a deep courtyard and incorporate still older buildings. A spacious entrance hall leads into a grand staircase hall; to the right is a handsome Drawing Room, to the left Library and Dining Room—the latter comprising one of the wide bows of the north front. There are fine chimneypieces and splendid plaster ceilings, and in one of the wings at the

back is a Gothick Catholic Chapel: the family took no notice of the Reformation, and have always been Papist. Anthony Salvin, the architect (much represented in the county), belonged to a junior, Anglican, branch. One of the great sights of Croxdale is the walled garden, nine acres in extent, which descends to a narrow lake and contains a great orangery. The mediaeval *church* (12th century and later) lies to the north among stable buildings: it is private property and the burial place of the family. The whole place is one of considerable romance, and seeming remoteness—albeit so close to the city, the railway, the roads, and industry, yet invisible to that other world, as that other world is invisible to it. The 13th-century *Sunderland Bridge* lies below the modern bridge (which carries the main road), and a rough track leads under the railway viaduct by the side of the river to *Holywell Hall*, a stone house of ancient origins. And along the main road are the gates to *Burn Hall*, a grand house built in 1821 by Bonomi, with great Ionic portecochère, the full height of the building, and walls of banded rustication. It was also a Salvin house, but is now a Roman Catholic seminary. There is a fine view of the house from the railway, and in the park charming farm buildings—the centre with pediment, the sidewings with pyramid roofs.

Dalton-le-Dale [11] Under the old A19, and its new dual carriageway which runs alongside, the road dips down to Dalton, with its collection of insignificant cottages—and, close by, the small blackened *parish church*. This is a simple but distinguished little Early English building, with bellcote and lancet windows. Visible only inside is a Norman north doorway, surviving from the earlier building. On the north wall inside, and perhaps unique, are the numerals VII to I cut into the stone, which represent

a curious sundial, the time of day being indicated by a sunbeam breaking through a window in the wall opposite. Two mediaeval effigies, one of a knight bearing the arms of Bowes—probably representing Sir William Bowes of Dawdon (Dalton) Tower. The road leads on down the wooded dene, past the remains of Dawdon Tower, to the outskirts of Seaham Harbour, called Dawdon—where there is a brick *church* of 1912 (by W. H. Wood), and an ugly smudge of miners' cottages, terrace upon terrace overlooking this disfigured coast.

Darlington [16] Every visitor to Darlington should arrive by train: not only is Darlington the spiritual home of all the railways of the world—and as such the pride of County Durham—it is also the ideal way of arriving. A mile south of Croft Bridge the railway line crosses the River Tees: 'YORKSHIRE' proclaims a great notice on the south side—'COUNTY DURHAM' another on the north. There is a glimpse of the river below, making its way wide and purposeful between green, wellwooded banks. The train slows down as it approaches the town, passes the junction with the historic line to Stockton, and enters *Bank Top Station*. Like a great church, with two parallel naves vaulted in iron, Bank Top Station, built in 1887, marks as it were the coming-of-age of the great railway system first pioneered here in 1825. Outside, a tall brick clock tower stands at the entrance to the covered courtyard, and it is an easy walk into the town itself. The great pleasure of Darlington is that it still preserves to an extraordinary degree the character of a large country town: the mediaeval parish church with its tall spire, the great market place, the covered market with its attendant clock tower and spire in Florentine Gothic (by Alfred

Burn Hall (*see* **Croxdale**)

Waterhouse), the 18th- and 19th-century houses and shops in High Row, the other streets and intimate alleys all around—these are the landmarks of the town. Crossing the new ring road and the little River Skerne hurrying on its way to join the Tees at Croft, we come to the *parish church* of St Cuthbert. The church stands simple and austerely beautiful at the lower end of the market place: cruciform with low central tower and tapering spire, it is a building in pure Early English style, with high pitched roof and tall lancet windows, built all of a piece by Bishop Pudsey in the closing years of the 12th century. He conceived it as the grand church of his important manor of Darlington—a collegiate church with Dean and four Canons. Stately

west front with two storeys of lancets and blind arcading; stately lofty nave with alternating round and clustered columns; lofty transepts repeating the theme of lancets and blind arcades—the chancel of equal height is solemn and mysterious, divided from the rest by stone screen or pulpitum. Powerful east end with three storeys of lancets (carefully rebuilt by Pritchett, 1864–5); Perpendicular Easter sepulchre; 15th-century stalls with misericords; Victorian mosaic reredos by John Dobbin, originally intended for Westminster Abbey; mediaeval font, with towering 'Cosin' font cover, in south transept. Among many tablets in the transepts the most interesting is to General Sir Henry Havelock, the hero of Lucknow. His son, General

Sir Henry Havelock-Allan, V.C., was also a distinguished soldier, who inherited Blackwell Grange (*see* p. 82) from the Allan family, to whom there are also memorials. On the other side of the ring road, north-east of St Cuthbert's, is *St Hilda's*. Of red brick, lofty with lancet windows, it was built in 1887 by J. L. Pearson: it is the 'high' church of the town. To the south-east stand the new *Fire Brigade headquarters*, and the new *Police station*; and the new *town hall* (designed by Williamson Fawkner-Brown of Newcastle, 1970) stands to the south of the parish church. The dual carriageway—however essential for relieving the inner town of the unceasing flow of traffic—and these new concrete blocks with the ever-present car parks, alas, make

79

△ Bank Top Station

▽ North Road Station

△ The Market Hall
Darlington

The Cummins Diesel factory, **Darlington**

something of a desert of this part of the town. The cooling towers and chimneys of the power station beyond form an inappropriate back-drop—but the prominent tower of *St John's Church* (at the corner of Neasham Road) is a more friendly landmark; with its lancet windows and Early English details, it was designed by the Darlington architect John Middleton, and the foundation stone was laid by George Hudson, the 'railway king', in 1847. Making our way across the *market place* we can note one or two pleasant 18th-century houses on the south side, and in Houndgate, behind, is *Pease House*, the home of Edward Pease (1787–1858), banker, Quaker, one of the promoters of the Stockton and Darlington railway. Next door is the old *Central Hall* (1847, by John Middleton) in an unpretentious

brick domestic Georgian style. There are more decent 18th-century houses on the other side of Houndgate. To walk along *High Row* and enjoy the 18th-century houses and shops, and Alfred Waterhouse's *Market Hall* and clock tower opposite, is a pleasure indeed: the clock tower gives enormous character to the town. Narrow alleys (such as Post House Wynd) connect with Skinnergate behind. *Barclays Bank* in High Row is an impressive Gothic building by Waterhouse (1864): it was originally the banking house of Messrs Backhouse, the other great Quaker banking family. And at the north end of High Row is the *statue of Joseph Pease*, Member of Parliament, Quaker, benefactor of the town (and donor of the clock tower), by A. Lawson (1875). Opposite, the *King's Head Hotel* is

High Victorian hotel architecture, the upper part of Woolworth's High Victorian Classical; but before proceeding up Northgate it is worth descending Priestgate (by the King's Head) to see the *Edward Pease Library* at the corner of Crown Street, a red-brick Renaissance affair by G. G. Hoskins of Darlington (1885). The ring road cuts across Northgate: a roundabout, a pedestrian subway, pedestrian precincts and recent glass and concrete blocks are the new landmarks here; but beyond all this are several worthwhile buildings. At the corner of Gladstone Street is the *Technical College* (by G. G. Hoskins, 1896) in deep red brick and golden terracotta; beyond that *Northgate Lodge*, a charming bow-fronted house of 1830, once the home of John Beaumont Pease; opposite, and equally charming, *no. 156*, an

18th-century house with wide pediment and bay windows. The *United Reform Church* has a blackened spire; opposite is the *Salvation Army Citadel*—and the road leads on to that most notable railway shrine, North Road Station (turn left before the railway bridge). *North Road Station* is the historic terminus of the Stockton and Darlington railway. It was built in 1842: with its cream-washed stucco, sash windows and cast-iron colonnade it has a domestic appearance, and could pass as a minor country house. It has been beautifully done up in recent years, and is now an important railway museum. Here it is possible to see Stephenson's Locomotion Nº 1, and other early engines and carriages—all splendidly preserved. Retracing our steps down Northgate, and turning west into Bondgate, *no. 81* is a distinguished early 19th-century classical stone house (now the offices of Messrs Smiths Gore); and the *Britannia Inn* is of interest as the birthplace of J. M. Dent, the publisher and founder of Everyman's Library. The *Bondgate Methodist chapel* (in Salt Yard, next door to the Majestic Bingo Hall) is a handsome Classical building (1814), with later Lombardized windows. And a little further down, in Woodlands Road (corner of Vane Terrace) is *Holy Trinity*, by Salvin (1838), in its quiet, retired churchyard. But Skinnergate leads south (parallel with High Row), and at the south end stand the *Mechanics' Institution* (Victorian Classical in brick, by J. P. Pritchett, 1853) and, opposite, the *Friends' Meeting House* (1840) with its dignified brick façade—the Peases and Backhouses and other eminent Darlington families were Quakers in the 18th and 19th centuries. In Blackwellgate and Coniscliffe Road are some charming early 19th-century brick terraces; and set back behind the houses is St Augustine's *R.C. church*, in its quiet garden with presbytery and school. Designed by

Bonomi in 1827 in Perpendicular style, with wide aisleless nave and narrow chancel—with a small altar on either side of the chancel arch—a towering High Altar with marble gradines and canopied reredos, with pitch pine pews and panelling, and a west gallery, it is a moving, devout interior. Good early Victorian (and later) houses lead on and out of the town westwards. One final landmark which may be mentioned is the 'Industrial Gothic' pumping house of the *Darlington Waterworks*, close to the river on the outskirts of the town. Blackwellgate leads south, lined with attractive Victorian houses, to *Blackwell Grange*. Seen from the road, an old avenue of limes frames the east front, a handsome early 18th-century façade with sash windows and parapet lined with urns. The house has been much extended and is now the Europa Lodge Hotel: here in 1973 Mr William Whitelaw held his Ulster Conference. It was the home of the Allans and Havelock-Allans, whose memorials are in the parish church. There are good chimneypieces and other original fittings within. And so to the river, where *Blackwell Bridge*, by John Green of Newcastle (1832), with its three arches carries the road across the Tees into Yorkshire.

Denton [16] Small village of whitewashed farm buildings and cream-washed cottages close to the Cocker Beck, a few miles north of the Tees; the lane leads through a 'villagescape' of barns and textured walls to one larger farmhouse (Denton Hall), and a diminutive *church* with bellcote and lancet windows (by Pritchett, 1891), containing a 14th-century effigy of a member of the Conyers family in a cupboard in the vestry. Walled orchards beyond—until the lane peters out. Half a mile to the west the Roman road from Piercebridge (B6275) makes its way north: near the crossroads, two miles on, stands

Legs Cross, an Anglo-Saxon wayside cross, set on a Roman stone—the name perhaps a corruption of the Latin *Legio*.

Dinsdale, Low [17] The lower Tees valley at its lushest, most secretive and most beautiful. The narrow road from Neasham leads inconsequently, meanderingly, to this tiny hamlet: the river running north from the Sockburn peninsula suddenly turns west, then east, then south again, making its slow and stately way towards the coast. Across these double loops there is a glimpse of Middleton One Row—but there is no way across to Middleton; the road, crossing the river by a narrow bridge, makes its way instead with sudden strange perversity south into Yorkshire, down many twisting turns to Yarm. Dinsdale is romantic, too, as the cradle of one of County Durham's most ancient, gifted and prolific families, the Surtees. Descended from Siward, who settled here in the early 12th century, the family adopted the name of 'Supra Teysam' or Sur-Tees, and flourished here till the early 16th century, when Thomas Surtees (who died childless in 1510) was succeeded by his sister who married John Place of Halnaby in Yorkshire. The Place family thrived here till the early 18th century, but after two further changes of ownership Dinsdale was repurchased by a Surtees in 1840—a descendant of a junior branch. The most distinguished member of the family was Robert Surtees of Mainsforth (1779–1834), the historian of County Durham, after whom the Surtees Society, the learned local history society, is named; he was the author of the four volumes of the *History of Durham*. The scion of another branch, Robert Smith Surtees of Hamsterley, was the creator of Jorrocks (*see* Mainsforth and Hamsterley). Nothing remains above ground of the mediaeval castle of

the Surtees, though fragments of it may be incorporated in the small 16th-century *manor house*, which stands, accompanied by dry moats, to the south-west of the church, a house of stone and timber, a building of charm. The little *church* of red sandstone, in origin 12th century, was much restored in 1875. In the porch is a 14th-century incised grave-cover, marked Gureslynus Surtees (Goselyne Surtees, d. 1366): in the Surtees chapel are tablets to the later members of the family. The interior is dark with rich Victorian glass by O'Connor. The discovery of a sulphur spring in the early 19th century led to the establishment of Dinsdale Spa, with baths near Middleton St George—and the spa-like village of Middleton One Row came into existence. *Dinsdale Park*, a plain handsome mansion by Bonomi (1829) nearer to Middleton, became a medical institution in the middle of the 19th century.

Dipton [3] Scattered housing all along the A692 from Consett to Whickham, and wide views over wooded country towards Hamsterley Hall to the north, and industrialized country to the south. The *church* is a small but stately building of 1874, cruciform with squat central tower: lying below and surrounded by farmland is *Pontop Hall*, a plain stone house of c. 1700, whose chief interest is that in the 18th century it housed the Roman Catholic seminary that is now the great college of Ushaw (q.v.). A mile further west along the main road towards Leadgate is a prominent and imposing *R.C. church*, with attendant presbytery, testifying to the old and important Catholic community in these parts. Indeed its prominence gives an unexpected continental air to this bleak, forbidding countryside.

◁ **At Denton**

Durham [10] For many people the first (or perhaps only) sight that they have had of Durham is the view from the railway. It is one of the most breathtaking views in the world. The railway, raised on its viaduct above the streets and houses of the city, commands an amazing prospect of the cathedral and castle: a few seconds later it is gone, but the sudden sight of this dominating, domineering citadel is one that can never be forgotten. For the visitor arriving in Durham by road there are several splendid first views of the cathedral: approaching the city from the north by the A690 (from the motorway), after passing the roundabout in Gilesgate, there is a grand vista of cathedral and castle from the north-east as the new road descends to the river; approaching from the south by the A167 (the old Great North Road) and forking right at the Cock o' the North (A1050) the towers of the cathedral appear above the trees and houses of Church Street as it descends into New Elvet. But the best approach of all is to turn left at the traffic lights before entering Church Street, look out carefully for the secret tree-laden approach to Pimlico and South Street on the right (just after the gate and lodge that lead to Prebends' Bridge), and enter the city here. After a short distance the cathedral comes in sight, at first half screened by the trees on the top of the river bank—then revealed in all its glory across the deep ravine of the River Wear. Here the visitor will wish to stand and stare—at the three great towers, at the Galilee Chapel at the west end, at the monastic buildings and the houses of the college to the south, at the castle and its attendant buildings to the north. From whichever way he may come, the visitor should abandon a car at the approach to the city: its narrow streets and cobbled alleys are best traversed on foot. So, descending South Street here it is possible to visit *St Margaret's church* (outwardly

Perpendicular, with battlemented, pinnacled west tower—but with Norman south arcade). Crossing Framwellgate Bridge and ascending Silver Street (now a pedestrian way) we enter the market place. The *Market Place* is dominated by the equestrian *statue of the 3rd Marquis of Londonderry* (by R. Monti, 1861)—known affectionately as 'the horse'. On the north side stands *St Nicholas's church* (rebuilt by Pritchett, 1857), on the west the *town hall* (by P. C. Hardwick, 1851). The narrow street in the south-east corner—Saddler Street—leads up to North and South Bailey, and by Owengate on to Palace Green. Stand on Palace Green: behind you is the *castle*, on the left *Bishop Cosin's Hall*, a tall square early 18th-century house with a grand doorway; this and the other buildings that line the Green are now all used by the University: Lecture Rooms beyond Cosin's Hall, and the *Old Grammar School*, the *Union Building*, the *University Library* and *Bishop Cosin's Library* on the side opposite. But the great sight is the full length of the north side of the cathedral. *Durham Cathedral* is the greatest Norman church in England: it was begun in 1093 and completed in 1133; only the Galilee Chapel at the west end (c. 1170), the east transepts or Chapel of Nine Altars (c. 1242), and the central tower (c. 1465, the upper stage c. 1490) being later additions. We enter by the north-west door (with its 12th-century knocker) to receive the first impact of the Norman nave. The great piers of the arcade, alternately circular and compound, patterned or plain, the triforium above with its own arcaded openings, the clerestory above that with windows set in their deeply arched recesses, each section of the nave divided from the next by its transverse arch—the whole vaulted with the earliest rib vault in Europe—the impact is tremendous. The eye is carried on and up, past the central crossing, through

The Market Place, **Durham**: St Nicholas' church and 'The Horse'

to the chancel, and so to the delicate Gothic of the east end. At the west end of the nave stands Cosin's marble font (1663) under its towering canopy—the finest single piece of all his church furnishings. Against the south wall of the south aisle has been re-erected the front of the 1683 organ case, which originally stood on the chancel screen which was removed in 1846. Moving east we come to the crossing: stand under the tower, and see where the highly decorative Perpendicular work meets the solid, simpler Norman arches which form the base of the tower. In the south transept is an exotic and wonderful *clock*, originally erected in the early

16th century, remodelled in the 17th, banished in the 19th, and re-erected in the 20th. Standing on marbled shafts, the great clock face, gilded and painted, is supported by elaborate pinnacles, then crowned by an open dome surmounted by a lofty finial. At the base the panels are painted with the interiors of a Dutch-like church. It is theatrical, delightful. Gilbert Scott's marble *pulpit* and *chancel screen* (1876) are more earnest and sober: the screen, in Florentine Gothic, proves a remarkably successful counterfoil to the Norman austerity of its setting, and a rich and dignified entrance to the choir. The *choir* presents a scene of remarkable

richness. Against the pale background of the Norman arcades Cosin's rich dark stalls stand out in magnificent splendour; to the east on the south side is the painted and gilded *tomb of Bishop Hatfield* (d. 1333), the effigy of the bishop under an arch below, the episcopal *throne* surmounted by a pinnacled arcade and canopy above, a unique arrangement, providing the Prince Bishops with the loftiest throne in Christendom. A 17th-century staircase and gallery complete it. The easternmost bay of the sanctuary is Early English, part of the reconstruction of the east end in the mid 13th century. Behind the High Altar is the *Neville screen*, given by

John Lord Neville c. 1380. Though bereft of its statues it is of great beauty and elegance; behind it and above it hangs Comper's colourful tester over St Cuthbert's shrine, which is immediately behind the High Altar. The *Chapel of the Nine Altars* provides a remarkable Gothic climax to the Norman church: tall shafts of Frosterley marble, long narrow lancet windows, elegant arcading, take the place of rugged columns and small round-headed windows; the floor is actually nearly six feet lower than the chancel—providing greater height. And on a raised feretory is the *tomb of St Cuthbert*, a simple stone slab on the site of the vanished mediaeval shrine. The *Galilee Chapel* at the west end is in the very latest Norman style, with slender columns supporting round arches generously adorned with zigzag carving. The chapel comprises nave, with double aisles each side—each aisle carries a low timber roof—and larger windows with Decorated or Perpendicular tracery flood the whole chapel with light; from the west windows is a dramatic view of the river below. It is a remarkable building of many vistas: in the inner south aisle is the simple *tomb of the Venerable Bede*, supported by four baroque gilt candlesticks. The *cloisters* lie on the south side of the cathedral: Norman and mediaeval in origin, they were much rebuilt in the 18th and 19th centuries, and the tracery of the windows is charmingly Gothick. On the west side is the *Monks' Dormitory* (upper floor): this is now the Cathedral Museum, and contains notable treasures—such as St Cuthbert's pectoral cross, removed from his coffin when it was opened in 1827; and important illuminated manuscripts. In the south-west corner of the cloisters is the recently opened *Cathedral Treasury*, in which a collection of plate from the cathedral and diocese is displayed. Opposite is the excellent Cathedral Restaurant:

Durham is the only English cathedral in the *Good Food Guide*. On the south side of the cloisters is the *Refectory*, converted into the Cathedral Library in the 17th century, and with its contemporary bookcases resembling a college library at Oxford or Cambridge. On the south wall of the cloisters is the monument to John Meade Falkner, author and antiquary (*The Lost Stradivarius*, *The Nebuly Coat*, etc.). On the east side is the *Chapter House*, largely rebuilt in 1895. In the south-east corner a narrow alley leads through to College Green; but at this stage it may be best to return to Palace Green and visit the castle. *Durham Castle* was begun soon after the Conquest, and was shortly afterwards bestowed by the Conqueror on Bishop Walcher, the first Prince Bishop. It was an important fortress against the Scots, and also the principal residence of the bishop—and so remained until Bishop van Mildert bestowed it on the newly founded university (1832), when it became University College. The *gatehouse* is in toy-fort Gothick by James Wyatt (or perhaps Carr of York: there is conflicting evidence), but the archway itself is of Norman origin. Through this the courtyard is entered: on the left is the Great Hall, built in the 13th and 14th centuries by Bishops Bek and Hatfield; in the north-west corner the extruding tower contains Cosin's *Black Staircase*; the north side is the 12th-century building of Bishop Pudsey, though the façade was rebuilt in the 18th by Bishop Trevor with Gothick upper windows, and the lower section concealed by the 16th-century gallery built by Bishop Tunstall, who also built the clock tower and chapel. On the right is the *Keep*, standing on its motte; this was rebuilt by Salvin in 1840—J. C. Buckler's watercolour (1800) shows the original keep in a ruinous condition. The *Great Hall* is entered by the grand portico added by Bishop Cosin after the Restoration:

Durham Cathedral: the west front

pp 90 and 91 the nave ▷

his coupled Ionic columns and flight of stone steps make an imposing entrance. The Hall is now the Dining Hall of the College; here hang portraits of eminent university figures. Bishop Cosin's *Black Staircase* adjoins the dais, and leads up to *Tunstall's Gallery*: on the north side of this are what were the Bishop's State Rooms, and are now the Senior Common Room of the college. It is odd to approach these handsome 18th-century rooms through a rugged Norman doorway. On the top floor is the *Norman Gallery*—the original Norman arcades lit by Bishop Trevor's Gothick windows. At the end of Tunstall's Gallery is his *chapel*, now the College Chapel, dating from 1540, and containing some contemporary stalls and panelling, and a 17th-century organ. A spiral staircase leads down to the *Norman Chapel* in the undercroft. This little chapel (supplanted in the 16th century by Tunstall's chapel) is the final jewel of Durham Castle. It is tiny and windowless: six stone columns, with intriguingly sculptured capitals, divide the central space from the diminutive aisles; the beautiful marking of the honey-coloured stone is a special delight. Unused for centuries, the chapel has recently been restored to use, and contains the simplest of furnishings. It is a holy place. All along the wooded bank of the river on this east side is a secluded walk, and it is possible to descend by the narrow alley which leads off Palace Green next to the University Library (the New Library is by G. G. Pace, 1967); on the other side a plaque records that the house here was the home of John Meade Falkner. The walk under the west front of the cathedral, past the old Mill on the river, is romantic: there are views up and downstream to

The Galilee Chapel

The nave ▷

The Neville screen

Framwellgate Bridge and Prebends' Bridge—and perched on
the opposite bank are the houses in
South Street. Climbing up, there is
a mysterious tunnel called the *Dark
Entry* which leads into College
Green. Smaller, more intimate
than Palace Green, it forms a long,
enclosed court around which are
the houses of the canons (several of
whom, as at Christ Church, are
also Professors). The south side is
lined with charming 18th-century
houses, built on the site of monastic
buildings, with steps and iron
hand-rails leading to their front

doors. In the south-west corner is
the *Choir School*, stuccoed and
Gothick (but containing a 17th-
century staircase). On the west side
stands an octagonal *Conduit House*
(1751), and behind it the *Registry*,
castellated and stuccoed (early
19th century). The old monastic
kitchen abuts the south side of the
cloisters (now used for the
cathedral archives), and, next to
this, the *Deanery*, which was formerly the Prior's Lodging—its
Georgian sash windows masking
the mediaeval building and the
Prior's Hall. Next to the Deanery is

the most charming of all the houses
(the residence of the Chapter
Clerk) with two-storeyed front and
arched 18th-century windows, and
short projecting wings. We leave
College Green by *Prior Castell's
Gatehouse* (c. 1510) into the Bailey.
North and South Bailey constitute
the most charming street in the
city: narrow and secluded, it
stretches from Saddler Street to
Prebends' Bridge in a gentle,
informal arc. Turning right, outside the gatehouse, we can make
our way down to the river, pausing
at the little church of *St Mary-the-*

The font cover

Less, now the chapel of St John's College: a rebuilding (by Pickering, 1846) of the original Norman church, and containing some Norman features, an early 13th-century sculptured relief of Christ in the chancel, and some 17th-century 'Cosin' woodwork. Through the Watergate we reach *Prebends' Bridge* (by George Nicholson, 1778), and looking north can savour the view downstream, with the towers of the cathedral above the wooded bank of the river. Inscribed on the balustrade are Scott's lines:

Grey towers of Durham, Yet well I love thy mixed and massive piles, / Half church of God, half castle 'gainst the Scots.

Turning back, we can enjoy the varied houses in the Bailey—some brick, some stuccoed, some stone. The most distinguished is 3 South Bailey, now *St John's College*, the former Eden town house, a three-storeyed stone house of 1730, with banded rustication and a stately doorway. Opposite the east end of the cathedral is *St Chad's College*, with an attractive new building by

Francis Johnson (1965) at the corner of Bow Lane, which includes a new Dining Hall; behind the 18th-century houses on the street Mr Johnson has devised a small enclosed quadrangle. Next to St Chad's is the church of *St Mary-le-Bow*, a little building of 1685, with early 18th-century tower, the interior containing a feast of 17th-and 18th-century woodwork. A little further on is *Hatfield College* (founded 1846, the second oldest college of the university). The original building is the former Red Lion Hotel, a spacious 18th-century brick house. To this have been added Tudor stone buildings by Salvin (1848) and a Gothic chapel, and later 20th-century blocks (by Vincent Harris, 1950) in a scholarly Georgian idiom in stone. The street merges with Saddler Street, where the procession of attractive, modest houses continues—notice *no. 50* with its Doric doorpiece, now the H.Q. of the Salvation Army. In so many instances a Georgian façade conceals an earlier house; many contain good, and often earlier, features—particularly staircases. Mr Francis Johnson has produced a small book *Historic Staircases in Durham City* (City of Durham Trust, 1970), in which many of these are listed. And so we are back in the market place. The new relief road passes underneath, beyond St Nicholas's Church: in a prominent position towards the station is the R.C. church of *Our Lady of Mercy and St Godric* (by E. W. Pugin, 1864), with its big west tower and apsidal chancel, the interior lavishly and gaily decorated. Near the railway viaduct the main roads divide. The A690 (to Crook) leads up to *Neville's Cross* (the stump of the cross marks the victory over the Scots at the Battle of Neville's Cross in 1346), the A691 (to Lanchester) passes *St Cuthbert's*, a Victorian church by E. R. Robson (1857) with saddleback tower; nearby is the tall obelisk of the Observatory Meridian (1850). But turning back, and crossing the river by the new bridge, we come to the old *Elvet Bridge* (now pedestrianized)—which leads back to Saddler Street. Old Elvet leads to the east—a wide street of stately 18th-century houses, beginning with the *Royal County Hotel*, with its Ionic pilasters; the former *Shire Hall* (1898, by H. Barnes and F. E. Coates) in the reddest of red brick is something of an intrusion. Near the end of the street, and across a green, is the *Assize Court* (1809, by Francis Sandys), a long, stately

building with Tuscan portico and cupola. Hard by is the *R.C. church of St Cuthbert* (1827 by Bonomi) with low tower and attractive early 19th-century Gothic interior, the sanctuary adorned with the arms of old local recusant families who fostered the mission in early days. There was a strong Popish tradition in Durham; Defoe in his *Tour through England and Wales* (c. 1715) describes the city as 'full of the Catholicks who live peaceably and disturb nobody and nobody them, for we saw them going as publicly to their Mass as the Dissenters to their meeting house'. New Elvet leads south, past the *Three Tuns Hotel*, and both here and in Church Street beyond are many decent Georgian houses. But first, on the right are new university buildings—*Dunelm House*, and *Elvet Riverside* (by Architects' Co-Partnership, 1965). The new footbridge—*Kingsgate Bridge*—by Ove Arup (1963) across the river here leads over to North Bailey. In Church Street is *St Oswald's*: outwardly all Perpendicular (except for the elaborate Victorian east end (1864)), the three east bays of the nave are late Norman. There are 15th-century stalls, and a number of pleasant small monuments. The west window is by Ford Maddox Brown (made by Morris & Co., 1864); a window, by Kempe, in the north aisle commemorates Hodgson Fowler, architect (d. 1910), who worshipped in the church. St Oswald's was the scene of the ministry (1862–75) of J. B. Dykes, the hymnologist (*Hymns Ancient and Modern*), a pioneer of the Catholic revival here, persecuted by the Evangelical Bishop Baring. For the visitor who wishes to explore the new colleges it will be necessary to take to a car, and drive south beyond St Oswald's. Beyond the traffic lights, in South Road, are the buildings of the university science departments. The main building of pale brick (by Professor J. S. Allen, 1951) has a certain grandeur, in a

modern idiom. The *Science Library* nearby is by William Whitfield (1965), and the *Department of Psychology* building, also by William Whitfield (1970), received a Civic Trust Commendation. Opposite, *St Mary's College* by Vincent Harris (1952) is a scholarly neo-Georgian composition, with hipped roof and sash windows. Further south are *Grey College* (1960 by Thomas Worthington), on high ground beyond the science buildings; and *Collingwood College* (by Richard Sheppard, Robson & Partners, 1973) in a beautiful position overlooking the meadows. On the west side of the main road stands *Trevelyan College* (by Stillman and Eastwick-Field, 1967), and *van Mildert* (by Middleton Fletcher & Partners, 1966), with its tall concrete blocks overlooking lake and fountain. To the west again stands *St Aidan's* (by Sir Basil Spence, 1965) in a magnificent position, with a fine view south from its long loosely composed wings; and from the Hall, at the centre of the building, a great prospect of the cathedral to the north. And nearby (approached by Elvet Hill Road) is the *Gulbenkian Museum of Oriental Art* (by Middleton Fletcher & Partners, 1961), which contains an important collection of Egyptian antiquities (largely formed by the 4th Duke of Northumberland in the 19th century), a unique collection of Chinese jade, and a collection of Chinese porcelain formed by Mr Malcolm MacDonald, the present Chancellor of the University. Beyond all this, on the main road (A1050) is *Mount Oswald*; the park is the golf course, the mansion an imposing early 19th-century neo-Classical building, with a long façade of sash windows and Doric pilasters. Returning to the traffic lights and turning left, we shall find in Margery Lane, above South

Path from the College and grand doorways, Durham ▷

96

Street, *Durham School*. The origins of the school, as part of the cathedral foundation, are extremely ancient. It was refounded in 1541, and its original building on Palace Green, close to the west end of the cathedral, is now the Music Department of the university. As the school evolved from ancient grammar school to modern public school it outgrew the old building; the new school was designed by Salvin in 1844, and to this nucleus Sir Arthur Blomfield added the library (1876) and further ranges of buildings (1884). The most imposing building is the chapel by Walter Brierley (1926), which stands on its high grassy bank, approached by a long flight of steps. It remains to return to Elvet Bridge, and explore Claypath and Gilesgate, to the north-east. The long uphill street contains many pleasing old houses; just past the post office there is a glimpse of *Crook Hall*, a complete mediaeval manor house, masked by a 17th-century façade, with a taller 18th-century wing alongside. On the opposite side of the street, Leazes Place is a charming early 19th-century cul-de-sac, lined on either side with small terrace houses. Half-way up the hill is the roundabout, at the intersection of the A690; below is the *College of St Hild and St Bede*, with its chapel (1939) by Seely and Paget. Beyond the roundabout the street becomes almost a long village green, with *St Giles's church* set back on the right. The church presents a venerable Norman face to the north, with small Norman windows high up in the wall; there is much Norman work inside, but the south aisle is 19th century. In the sanctuary is the wooden effigy of John Heath (1591), the friend of Bernard Gilpin (*see* Houghton-le-Spring). He acquired the *Kepier Hospital* after the dissolution; its 14th-century

left and opposite **Durham**: streetscapes near the cathedral

gateway survives, close to the river to the north, though little of the Elizabethan house which he built beside it. From St Giles's church-yard we bid farewell to the city: from the high ground here, partially screened by trees, is a final view of cathedral and castle, in all their splendour.

Easington [11] Travelling from the north, the *church* appears prominent on its hill: there is a gentle ascent from the roundabout on the dual carriageway, and the church stands perched high in its church-yard—with wide views over cottages and collieries to the cold North Sea. Stately Early English church with clerestoried nave, and long chancel, the embattled west tower dating from the Norman period. Inside, it is richly furnished with 'Cosin' style pews: Denis Granville, Cosin's son-in-law, was indeed rector here after the Restoration. Low screen, chancel stalls, reredos all add to the seemly 17th-century atmosphere. The east end, with its five lancets, is a scholarly reconstruction of c. 1850; the stained glass is by O'Connor. Opposite stands the former *rectory*, now an old people's home, clearly a house of great antiquity with its buttressed front and medley of sash and (at the back) mediaeval windows. Easington was a rich living. Round the church is the usual hotchpotch of old village—terrace houses, new bungalows, a public house; the road leads down towards the sea to Easington Colliery.

Easington Colliery [11] This was the scene in May 1951 of the most terrible mining disaster of modern times. An explosion occurred in the Five Quarter seam that killed or

◁ In the Castle Chapel, **Durham**

Wooden effigy of John Heath in St Giles' church (*top*)
St Cuthbert's coffin in the cathedral ▷

◁ Detail of Cosin woodwork in
Egglescliffe

entrapped over eighty men. The
tragedy is commemorated in the
church. The *Church of the Ascension* is
an agreeable plain brick building of
1928, in a modified Gothic mode;
the interior has been gorgeously
decorated by Sir Ninian Comper in
memory of the victims of the disaster, and is brilliant with Comper's
rich colours and gilding in screen
and altar, against a background of
white walls. The church stands in
Seaside Lane—a misnomer
suggesting seaside hotels, cafés and
amusements. Seaside Lane in
Easington is merely the main
street, off which run row upon row
of drab red-brick cottages, back to
back, front to front; supermarkets
and bingo halls and public houses
abound—and all around hangs the
acid atmosphere of coal. It is a grim
but cheerful place. A number of
eminent politicians have represented Durham constituencies in
recent years; Emanuel Shinwell
(Lord Shinwell) was Member for
Easington for twenty-five years.

East Boldon *see* Boldon

East Rainton *see* Rainton

Eastgate [8] The splendid moorland scenery of Weardale, on the
road from Stanhope to Alston, is
rudely punctuated here by the large
and obtrusive cement works.
Smoke belches from a tall chimney,
and trees and hedges and walls are
powdered with white dust. But the
great bare moors rise supreme on
either side; a gathering of houses
comprises the village, and a good-
looking neo-Perpendicular *church*
(by J. Johnson, 1887) lies a little
way off the main road, on a lane
that leads up to the moors by a
rushing moorland stream, and
peters out. *Westernhopeburn* is a

At **Egglescliffe** (*top*) ▷

At **Eggleston**

above and opposite **Egglestone Abbey**

hamlet on the other side of the Wear: there is one long low stone house of 1601.

Ebchester [3] The Roman road from York to Hadrian's Wall crossed the Derwent here: to guard the crossing the fort of Vindomora was established, and the church and churchyard occupy the south-west corner of the fort. Roman fragments are built into the tower of the church and other local buildings. The village stands astride the A694, in wooded country close to the Northumberland frontier. The *church* was largely

rebuilt in the last century, but it is in essence a small Norman building with Norman (or quasi-Norman) features. Exceedingly dark interior. R. S. Surtees, the creator of Jorrocks, who lived at Hamsterley Hall (q.v.) is buried in the churchyard close to the south side of the church: his widow is commemorated in the west window of the church.

Edmondbyers [3] A lonely spot in high moorland country, with views everywhere across a landscape of heather and sheep. The road to Blanchland skirts the Derwent

Reservoir (completed in 1967) and passes *Roughside Hall*, a Georgian shooting box on the banks of the great lake. This was the home of Colonel D. Clifton-Brown, Speaker of the House of Commons 1943–51, who was created Lord Ruffside. Small Norman *church*, with a great cock on the little bellcote, somewhat restored in the 19th century, but exceedingly pretty in its wellplanted churchyard. The interior is very dark with Victorian glass, and contains much 17th-century woodwork from Durham Cathedral, Auckland Castle and St Mary Redcliffe.

Egglescliffe [17] The River Tees twists and turns on its silvery way, dividing County Durham from the North Riding, Egglescliffe from Yarm. The river is crossed by the 15th-century bridge, and the great railway viaduct of forty-three arches, built in 1849, carrying the line from Northallerton to Stockton. Egglescliffe village is a cul-de-sac, approached by a turning off the main road (A19)—a typical Durham village of cottages surrounding a many-sided green. Delightful Perpendicular *church*, with battlemented west tower, battlemented nave and south aisle, the south doorway and chancel arch surviving from an earlier building. The interior is distinguished with its array of 'Cosin' woodwork: screen, pews, chancel stalls—and an 18th-century three-decker pulpit. The churchyard stands high on the north bank of the river, and there are views over the charming little town of Yarm, with its cupola-crowned town hall; in the churchyard a magnificent 19th-century pinnacled Gothic monument, and many good headstones. A mile to the north is Eaglescliffe Junction on the Stockton and Darlington line, with an industrial estate and a rash of cottages and villas.

Eggleston [15] On the road from Barnard Castle to Middleton-in-Teesdale: the countryside becomes wilder, and the sense of excitement grows. Small village, with 17th-century bridge across the Tees: *Eggleston Hall*, close to the river and embowered in trees, is an early 19th-century stone house by Bonomi, with Doric colonnade on the ground floor—built by the Hutchinson family. There is a view of the house from the higher ground across the river. In the grounds are the ruins of the little early 18th-century church: the Victorian *church* (1859) stands outside the Hall gates: well-furnished, comfortable interior.

Egglestone Abbey [15] In an idyllic position, where the Thorsgill Beck runs into the Tees; the road from Rokeby crosses the river by the Monks' Bridge, and a lane leads up to the Abbey. There are glimpses of the ruins through the trees, and suddenly the east end is above you, standing on its grassy knoll. The abbey was founded for Premonstratensian canons at the very end of the 12th century. The church is cruciform and aisleless, and much of nave and chancel survive—the chancel with elegant Early English double lancet windows. The east window with its mullions is perhaps 17th century: the monastic buildings were converted into a house after the dissolution, and the long range to the north with its Tudor mullioned windows looks like an Elizabethan manor house in ruins. Egglestone, with its farmhouse and simple cottages nearby, its stone walls and its wide views—with the river rushing below—seems indeed an enchanted spot: the stone mediaeval grave slabs, some beautifully carved, are reminders of its holiness.

Eldon [10] East of St Andrew Auckland, north of Shildon—an unpromising spot. There are brickworks, remains of an old colliery—'CAUTION: ROAD LIABLE TO SUBSIDENCE'—a Victorian church of small stones and small lancet windows, a railway embankment; all the usual ingredients of a run-down industrial village. A strange place (it seems now) for a great Lord Chancellor (1801) to take for his title.

Elton [17] Now bypassed by the Stockton–Darlington road. Early 20th-century Lutyensesque 'Queen Anne' *Hall*, built by the Ropners, and a small *church* rebuilt in 1841, with bellcote and (genuine) Norman features. Delightful interior with Comper roodscreen, gay and colourful.

Elwick [11] A pretty spot just off the A19 Sunderland–Stockton road: the village street with a green on either side of the road. The *church* stands on higher ground to the south-west. Early 19th-century tower on the south side, early 13th-century nave and aisles, 17th-century chancel, two small Saxon carvings on either side of chancel arch. The church stands in a delightful position.

Escomb [10] Renowned for its tiny Saxon *church*, 'after Durham Cathedral, the most impressive ecclesiastical building in the county' wrote Georgina Battiscombe (*Collins' Guide to English Parish Churches*, ed. by John Betjeman, 1958). It stands in unpromising surroundings: a squalid industrial valley, with council houses opposite. Tall narrow nave, narrow chancel, the chancel arch built of blocks of stone removed from the Roman fort at Binchester. The whole church breathes the atmosphere of early British piety of the age of Bede. Two or three larger windows are later insertions: otherwise the church is untouched since Saxon times. For a long time the church was unused, and a Victorian successor was built up the hill: as with the Saxon church at Bradford-on-Avon, Escomb has survived through being forgotten and neglected; but in recent years the Victorian church has been pulled down, and the old church brought back to life. It has been restored and refurnished, with great care and tact, by Sir Albert Richardson, P.R.A.

Esh [10] Hilltop village on the minor road from Durham to Lanchester: splendid late 17th-century gate piers, with scrolled finials supporting balls, lead to the *Hall*, now a farmhouse and a mere fragment (with a few 17th-century features) of the great house of the Smythe family, recusant baronets. The Smythes, of Durham extraction,

Esh Hall gate piers

acquired by marriage the property of Acton Burnell in Shropshire, which subsequently became their principal seat. They intermarried with all the prominent old recusant families—Haggerstons, Arundells, Blounts, Cliffords—but their most celebrated member was Maria Anne, granddaughter of the 3rd baronet, the great Mrs Fitzherbert, subsequently the wife of George IV. The *parish church* is small, dark and Victorian, though incorporating an older structure. Along the road to the west is the grander *R.C. church*: standing quite alone, it forms with the priest's house, a lodge and stable buildings a little open quadrangle. The large graveyard behind testifies to the flourishing old Catholic community fostered here by the Smythes.

Esh Winning [10] The 'back' road from Durham to Lanchester across the hills commands wide views—to other hills to the south, and to the moorlands beyond Tow Law to the west; nestling in the valleys below sudden little industrial villages appear. Such a one is Esh Winning, a mile or two south of Esh, a towny little place, grubby but winsome—with appealing little terraces of miners' cottages, and no building of any prominence but the 1930s Majestic Cinema. Old collieries around, Hamsteels, Cornsay, Waterhouses: for Durham atmosphere Esh Winning is not to be missed.

Etherley, High [9] The road north-west from West Auckland climbs to Toft Hill: the row of little terrace houses is dominated by a grim grey *Primitive Methodist chapel*

108

of 1879. Its sombre frontispiece, two tiers of orderly round-headed windows with an oeil-de-boeuf in the pediment and a date stone over the door, bears an almost Palladian seemliness—but the Lombardic tracery of the windows betrays its mid-Victorian date. The A68 leads on to Witton-le-Wear and Fir Tree, with vide views over Hamsterley Forest, but the A6073 leads to Etherley village itself. *Church* of 1833: solid west tower with large weather vane and painted cartouche of Bishop van Mildert's arms above the door; barn-like nave with long Perpendicular windows; conventional Victorian chancel; well-kept churchyard planted with beech trees, and handsome 19th-century Tudor *rectory* behind. *Etherley Lodge* is a mid-Victorian stone-gabled house with some entertaining chimneys.

Evenwood [15] Driving northeast from Staindrop from the rural scenery surrounding the River Tees, Evenwood is the first sight of industry. Typical Durham industrial village: Victorian *church* (1863).

Fatfield [4] Old village, now incorporated in Washington New Town: much new housing (*see* Washington). Fragments of the old village near the *church*, which overlooks the new dual carriageway (Washington Highway) in a prominent position—an imposing red-brick building (1879) with an elegant flèche, rather grander, and later in date, than those in many mining villages.

Felling [4] Terrace upon terrace, climbing the hillside facing the Tyne and across to Newcastle. The traffic on the dual carriageway (A184) moves ever faster to join the motorway or make for Sunderland; the High Street runs parallel on the higher ground above, between *Christ Church* (1866) by Austin and Johnson and *St Patrick's R.C. church*

(1893) by Charles Walker, two imposing Victorian buildings—the latter dominating the hillside. There is a town hall nearby, with French-like mansard roof and cast-iron corona, a police station, and a public park with neat municipal flower beds. In Crow Hall Lane is one tall 18th-century stone house, called *Crow Hall*; otherwise it is all a sea of Victorian housing. (*See also* Heworth.)

Fence Houses [4] Amorphous housing everywhere: there is a level crossing over the main road (A1052) with a charming Victorian *signal box* looking like a conservatory perched on a very high pedestal, and a Victorian *church* at Chilton Moor (1872). Somewhere in the midst of all this a farm track leads off the main road into open country. Trees screen farm buildings, and, here in the middle of nowhere, stands *Morton House*, a stone manor house of 1709 with a distinguished front door with a cherub's head and cartouche in the open pediment.

Ferryhill [10] That odd conglomeration of ugly housing which crowns a conspicuous hill on the old Great North Road between Rushyford and Durham, Ferryhill—with its terrace upon terrace of drab miners' cottages—is a prominent landmark, the old A1 driving under the town in a deep cutting, with bridges passing overhead. Until recently the enormous slag heap of the old Dean and Chapter Mine stood beside the main road: now it has been landscaped, and grass and trees have been planted up its gentle slopes. The transformation is incredible. Up the steep hill from the main road is a long narrow market place, with a little town hall at one end, the war memorial—the figure of a soldier—standing in front. Parallel with this is Church Lane: here stands the *church* (by Bonomi, 1843), with the usual bellcote and

lancet windows, more recent vestries added at the west end, and a simple, pretty interior. Further up the lane is the Gaiety Dance Hall, and the terrace of houses below is grandly called Kensington Gardens. The other steep hill descends to Ferryhill Junction, where the Stockton branch joins the main line.

Finchale Priory [10] A secret, secret place. There is a minor road from Durham itself which leads north direct to the *Priory*, close to the river; but the usual means of approach is by foot from the road that runs from the A167 to the A690. Finchale (pronounced 'Finkle') stands in a romantic, beautiful, solitary spot on the south bank of the River Wear, at a point where the river makes one of its customary sharp bends. Deep woods clothe the side of the hills to the north; a wicket gate (easily missed) on the road, a footpath through the woods down to the river, a footbridge across the river—and so to the priory itself. And the view of the ruins opens up only by degrees: from the footbridge the prospect of the river, up and downstream, and of the priory buildings ahead, is one not soon to be forgotten. It is a delectable spot. There is an unsophisticated little café, selling ice cream and postcards—otherwise it is farmland all round; although the city is only a few miles away, a motorway and the main railway line even nearer, colliery villages to left and right, it is still possible to appreciate the loneliness of the spot when St Godric first established his solitary hermitage here in the earliest years of the 12th century. St Godric died in 1170 (*aet.* 105): in 1196 the Benedictine priory was founded, and building proceeded throughout the first half of the 13th century. It was never a large establishment—there were fifteen monks towards the end of the century, and from the 14th century till the time of the dissolution Finchale was used as a rest-house for the monks of Durham. A prior and four monks formed the regular establishment, and every three weeks groups of four monks would come out to Finchale. For so small a community the buildings seem spacious indeed. The *church* itself is long and narrow—the choir longer than the nave—and for some reason unknown the aisles were pulled down in the 14th century (perhaps at the time when the priory was re-established as a rest-house) and the arcades were filled in. But the circular piers, with capitals with stiff-leaf carving and unusual pineapples and flowers, are visible; windows with Decorated tracery (unusually late for this type of tracery) were inserted

in the outer walls, and the south aisle of the nave became the north walk of the cloisters. There was a tower at the crossing which was still standing, crowned by a low spire, in the early 17th century, as shown by the engraving in Dugdale's *Monasticon* (1665): it had fallen by the time Buck made his drawing in 1728. There was a later (14th-century) tower south-west of the west front. East of the cloisters was the *Dormitory*, and opening from the south cloister, the *Refectory*—with the vaulted undercroft surviving, the vault resting on plain octagonal piers. The prior's house stood to the south of the choir. There are fragments of other minor buildings still standing, and the ruins are beautifully maintained by the Department of the Environment. Walking

across the soft grass there are views everywhere—through gaping windows or broken walls—to the hillside hung with woods, the River Wear running swiftly below.

Fishburn [11] A conspicuous smoking chimney—a sudden industrial eruption across the green fields near Sedgefield: flattened slag heap; miners' cottages; great coking works on the edge of the village.

Frosterley [9] Long Weardale village, with terrace houses and narrow back alleys. Frosterley marble has been quarried here for many centuries, and is to be found in churches all over the county. The *church* is by G. E. Street (1869)—his only work in the county—and with its broach spire is quiet and competent.

Gainford [16] is a lovely village—perhaps the most attractive of all the villages of County Durham. The main road from Darlington to Barnard Castle (A67) skirts it on its north side: the River Tees washes its south boundary. Entering the place from the east *St Peter's Roman Catholic school*, looking like a small Victorian reformatory, is an unexpected, even startling, introduction: thereafter the buildings of the village strike a more sober and indeed a delightful note, with 18th- and 19th-century cottages and larger houses jostling each other round the wide green, and along pretty terraces that protect the green from the main road, with high garden walls enclosing secret gardens from the outside world. At the south-west corner of the green stands the *church*, close to the river bank, and a charming, rugged composition with its low tower, 'engaged' aisles and wide roof embracing nave, aisles and chancel. There is no clerestory, but the interior is high and airy, with

Patchwork of crosses in the north porch of **Gainford** church

House groups, **Gainford** ▷

tall Early English arcades and lofty aisles, and spacious lofty chancel. The east end with its group of lancet windows and upper 'vesica' is impressive. The font is crowned with a Jacobean cover, and in the south aisle is a baroque monument of stone to John Middleton (1709), resplendent with garlands and cherubs; there are later smaller monuments to local gentry, for whom Gainford has been so long a place of residence—and indeed in the 19th century a spa. *Gainford Hall* stands north-west of the church, and is a tall, compact, striking stone manor house of 1603, built by an incumbent, the Revd John Cradock. The entrance front has a tall gabled central porch with a richly decorated front door; behind it is a balancing central gabled projection, and on the other fronts three equally lofty gables, with, again, a central projection. The roof is adorned with a row of eleven chimneys—and in the walled garden is a round stone dovecote. The house, which contains contemporary panelling and plasterwork, continued in the Cradock family till the mid-19th century, but it descended to farmhouse status, and became much decayed till its careful restoration and preservation in this century.

Gateshead [4] The Tyne, of course, is magnificent. But Gateshead has in recent years been ruined by monstrous tower blocks, the ancient town torn apart by 'relief' roads, dual carriageways, roundabouts, flyovers, underpasses: a concrete jungle indeed. There are, however, a few things to see. Close beside the Tyne Bridge (opened in 1928) and dwarfed by its single span steel arch, stands *St Mary's church* in its ancient, tree-lined churchyard, overlooking the river. The church is 14th century, the tower 18th, the interior richly furnished with 17th-century pews and chancel stalls. Under the tower is a baroque cartouche, with lions'

heads peering over the top, their claws grasping the sides, inscribed 'This steeple was rebuilt Anno Dom. 1740' and recording the four churchwardens' names. There are many monuments, some with touching inscriptions: one to Henry and George Barran, sons of a Mayor of Gateshead, 'who from the effects of fever caught during a tour of Greece and Italy died on the same day in Milan' (1851); another to John Shafto Hawks who died at Delhi 'of severe cold' (1844). The churchyard is full of atmosphere: there are great table tombs, looking like Jacobean dining tables; one blackened headstone close to the river commemorates James Craig, peruke-maker, who died in 1770; and there is a big square late 17th-century mausoleum to the Green family, designed by Robert Trollop, the Newcastle architect. The view across to the quayside of Newcastle and its many fine buildings adds to the appeal of this churchyard. In the High Street stands *Holy Trinity*: the south aisle, with its 13th-century front of lancets and arcading, is the former St Edmund's Chapel; the rest is a Victorian addition. A public house opposite is grandly called the *Metropole Hotel*; nearby is the *town hall*, blackened Lombardic—with a plain red-brick late Georgian house round the corner—now the housing office. A few good terraces across the way lead out towards Bensham. *St Cuthbert's* is a Victorian Norman church (1865), but *St Chad's* (1904), a little further west is an accomplished late Gothic building by W. S. Hicks. Prominent on its hillside, with octagonal central tower, transepts, and east Lady Chapel, the interior is equally imposing, and splendidly furnished—with glass in the Lady Chapel by Miss Townshend (1909). Further south, in Saltwell Park, is the romantic Gothic mansion, *Saltwell Towers*, built in 1860 for William Wailes, the stained-glass artist—now, alas, un-

occupied, its future uncertain; its gardens provide an uncommonly romantic public park. Further to the west in the valley of the little River Team is the *Team Valley Trading Estate*, established here in 1936 to provide new factories for the district at the time of the great depression of the 1930s in north-east England. It is notable as the first government-sponsored scheme of its kind, and its plan was the work of Lord Holford—though many other architects designed individual factories and buildings. There are factories big and small, built along the wide avenues, set in spacious surroundings. Close to the Durham Road, to the south, the *Shipley Art Gallery* (1915) is one of the few imposing public buildings in the town. And further south along the Durham Road is the *Whinney Hall Hospital*, an imposing Victorian house, once the home of the Joiceys—one of the great coal-owning families. It is worth taking the Old Durham Road (east of the Durham Road), and climbing up to Gateshead Fell. Here terrace after terrace, named after the heroes of the South African War—Kitchener Terrace, Baden-Powell Terrace, Methuen Terrace—date the growth of the town. At the top of the High Fell stands *St John's church* (1826) with its tall needle-like spire, which is such a prominent landmark—some of its details still Gothick. There is an old windswept churchyard; and, opposite the church, a lane named Sour Milk Hill Lane evokes the days when the Fell was a windswept village—and Gateshead but a modest town at its feet.

Gibside [4] The road south from the Tyne to Shotley Bridge (A694) is dreary indeed: long suburban growth extends to Rowland's Gill and beyond. But suddenly on the higher ground to the east is an unexpected sight: a tall column, surmounted by what appears to be a human figure, surrounded

St Mary's, **Gateshead**. Newcastle Cathedral and the Tyne Bridge beyond

by somewhat tattered wood-lands—with the shell of a great mansion standing above the steep bank of the Derwent. Such is the setting of Gibside. A National Trust signpost points to *Gibside Chapel*, and from a side road a drive leads up into the woods. An estate cottage or two, a walled garden, and so the drive leads on into the grassy enclosure which serves as the visitors' car park. A long wide avenue of Turkey oaks extends to right and left: at one end, on the right stands the chapel; on the left the avenue extends interminably (it seems), and leads the eye to the column at the other. At this point it is perhaps worth walking down the full length of the avenue towards the column, and drinking in the full

scale of what has been a noble lay-out—now (and for many years), alas, in decline. On the left, set back from the avenue, stands the *Orangery*, in ruins. At the far end the *Column*, which in the distance appears to terminate the avenue, is revealed still a long way off across a deep ravine. Below to the left is a glimpse of the ruined *mansion*: out of sight to the right are the *stables*, and (again invisible from here) the Gothick *Banqueting House*, also in ruins. It should be stressed that the rest of the estate is private, and not open to the public. Gibside, owned originally by the family of Marley, came by marriage to Roger Blakis-ton of Coxhoe in 1540. The Blakis-tons built the mansion in the early 17th century—with its mullioned

bay windows and porch with clas-sical columns, Jacobean coats of arms, and strap-work. Sir Francis Blakiston, 2nd Bt, had an only daughter Elizabeth, who married Sir William Bowes of Streatlam (q.v.)—and Gibside went to the Bowes family. Sir William's son, George Bowes, married Mary, daughter of Edward Cuthbert of St Paul's Waldenbury, Hertfordshire, who had created the great land-scape garden there; their daughter Mary Eleanor married John Lyon, 9th Earl of Strathmore—so the Strathmores inherited Gibside and St Paul's Waldenbury, and became Bowes-Lyon. The column, 140 ft. high, and higher than the Nelson column, is surmounted by a statue of British Liberty, carved by

Christopher Richardson (1757): the column is almost certainly by James Paine. Stables (1744), Banqueting House (1751) and (perhaps) the Orangery were designed by Daniel Garrett. Paine was architect of the *Chapel*, and work began on that in 1760. Walking back along the avenue we can appreciate Paine's design, inspired perhaps by Palladio's Villa Rotunda at Vicenza. An Ionic portico approached by balustraded steps to right and left, surmounted by parapet and balustrades adorned with urns, the square cruciform building is crowned with a low dome. The portico constitutes one arm of the cross: within, the other three are barrel-vaulted apsidal transepts, with Corinthian columns supporting the central drum, above which rises the low saucer dome. The altar, surrounded by communion rails, stands beneath the dome. Box pews stand in the four corners, and erect in the nave, facing the altar, stands a three-decker pulpit with sounding board looking rather like a Chinese umbrella. The vault-chamber beneath is the family mausoleum. George Bowes died in 1760, and Gibside passed to his daughter, the Countess of Strathmore. The Earl died in 1776, and she soon afterwards married a Captain Stoney, a 'penniless Irish adventurer', who tried to obtain all her property and ended up in prison. The full story is told in Ralph Arnold's *The Unhappy Countess* (Constable, 1957). Work on the chapel ceased, but the building was completed by her son, the 10th Earl, and consecrated in 1812. The furnishings and some of the decoration date from this time. It was he who remodelled the mansion, adding the north wing and battlemented parapet. The 10th Earl married his mistress, Mary Milner, on his death bed in 1820. Their son, named John Bowes, inherited all the Bowes property in County Durham, and was the founder of the Bowes Museum at Barnard Castle (q.v.). On his death in 1885 the property reverted to the Earls of Strathmore, and is still their property. The house was not lived in after the First War; the 16th Earl presented the chapel to the National Trust in 1965.

Great Lumley *see* Lumley, Great

Great Stainton *see* Stainton, Great

Greatham [11] (pronounced Greetham) Within a few miles of the industry of Hartlepool and Billingham; here in the great flat expanses at the mouth of the Tees salt has been produced for centuries. But Greatham is still a village. The long winding street leads to the parish church and the *Hospital of God*, founded by Robert de Stichill, Bishop of Durham, in 1272 'for forty poor brethren'. An informal group of buildings: across a wide lawn on the right the Hospital, by Jeffry Wyatville (1803), with its little Gothick clock tower and open Gothick arches leading to the hall—and a long wing of new dwellings for the inmates by Francis Johnson (1973); ahead, the *Master's House*, a sympathetic rebuilding of the earlier house (of 1725) by Francis Johnson. On the garden side its wide bow window overlooks a terraced garden, with a vista to open

Thorpe Farm, Greta Bridge

fields. Beneath the tower of the parish church is the *chapel* (1788), with its little bell turret; the interior (which had been Victorianized) has recently been refurnished with great charm by Francis Johnson. (The porch, a later addition and not by Mr Johnson, is unfortunate.) The *parish church* is largely a rebuilding of 1855 (west tower of 1909), but the attractive white interior is spacious, with stately 12th-century arcades.

Greta Bridge [15], supremely beautiful and simple, spans the River Greta with one elegant arch. It was designed by John Carr of York in 1773. A mile north the Greta, which has run parallel with the Roman road (A66) for so many miles, flows into the Tees. *The Morritt Arms Hotel*, with its long 18th-century face, three storeys high—a deservedly famous hostelry—stands on what is now a quiet back road, its sash windows overlooking the trees of Rokeby

Park: the main road now cuts across a corner of the park, leaving one pair of gates (with Grecian key frieze) seemingly marooned. A quiet lane leads to Brignall, another to Barningham. There is nothing else but the L-shaped 18th-century stone house close to the bridge, with its long attendant stables—and *Thorpe Farm*, at the corner of the road to Wycliffe, a chaste, Palladian stone house, with sash windows set in blind arcades: a small house of rare distinction.

Grindon [11] The road from Sedgefield to Stockton (A177) passes through green, rolling country; Grindon is a handful of cottages and—set back from the road—a ruined church of mediaeval date. It has been a ruin for a century and more.

Hamsterley [3] (N. Durham) A bleak former colliery village in wooded country near the Derwent, on the main road (A694) from

Whickham to Shotley Bridge: terrace houses, and a small 19th-century *church* hard by the road. But on the minor road (B6310) to Burnopfield, concealed by thick woods, accompanied by a grand railway viaduct (the extinct line from Newcastle to Consett), stand the elaborate Edwardian gates to *Hamsterley Hall*, a house of legendary interest as the home of that redoubtable Victorian squire, Robert Smith Surtees, the creator of Jorrocks. But architecturally, too, the house is of interest. It was built at the very end of the 18th century by Henry Swinburne, a younger brother of Sir John Swinburne of Capheaton (Northumberland), and an accomplished traveller and man of taste, in a delightful Strawberry Hill Gothick style. The main front is a simple castellated rectangle, with sash windows set in ogival frames, the windows themselves enlivened by lozenge glazing bars—Gothick 'at its prettiest, happiest best' as Mr Neville Whittaker has

Baptist detail, **Hamsterley** (in Weardale) ▷

remarked. The romantic park is beautifully planted, and the house stands at the end of a long drive which crosses a tributary of the Derwent. The house was bought in 1810 by Anthony Surtees, father of Robert: it was his daughter who married the 5th Viscount Gort, father of Field Marshal Lord Gort, V.C., who was Commander in Chief of the B.E.F. in France at the beginning of the Second World War, the hero of Dunkirk. But it was for many years the home of his younger brother (subsequently 7th Viscount)—and it was he who gave to Hamsterley a further charming and unexpected distinction by introducing to this south front a handsome Elizabethan bay and other mullioned windows from the great demolished house of Beaudesert in Staffordshire. Round the corner is the front door embellished by a magnificent early 18th-century doorcase with shell canopy, and at the back is another 18th-century doorway imported from a house in London. On the front lawn stands, as a garden ornament, a tall Gothic pinnacle from the Palace of Westminster, and at the side of the lawn a stone cupola from Beaudesert has become a garden temple. Inside there are further delights, some, à la Strawberry Hill, indigenous, some appropriate introductions: the 7th Lord Gort was an inveterate collector and man of taste. The house now belongs to the Field Marshal's granddaughter.

Hamsterley [9] (in Weardale) The industry of Witton Park and Toft Hill is but a few miles away to the east, but this is open country, with Hamsterley Forest stretching for mile after mile to the south-west. Long street of pleasant cottages bordering the green, and a charming Georgian Gothick *Baptist chapel*.

◁ **Hartlepool**

The *church* stands away from the village to the east, a small Early English building with a Norman south door and 17th-century bellcote. A mile to the west, upon the Bedburn Brook, stands *Bedburn Mill*, a tall early 19th-century water mill with stepped gable—derelict, but under restoration. A mile on, along the road to Wolsingham, is the playful cottage ornée lodge to *Hoppyland Hall*. The drive is grassed over, and Hoppyland, delightfully named, is but a ruined Gothick house of 1793, with castellated towers and turrets, beautiful and mellow in decay. The grounds include a derelict garden house, and across the rising parkland grass walks lead to a valley ablaze with rhododendrons in spring.

Hart [11] The mother church of Hart-le-pool. The village stands on rising ground, and there are wide views across the fields to the sea. The *church* is in substance Saxon, and there are Saxon fragments visible in the nave; the arcades are later insertions—the northern (and chancel arch) perhaps Transitional, the southern probably early 17th century; the chancel itself an early 19th-century rebuilding. The tower is Norman. Interior scraped, but full of atmosphere; two fonts—one plain Norman, one ornate 15th century. West of the church is one wall of the ancient manor house, with one mediaeval window.

Hartlepool [11] The sight of Old Hartlepool across the bay—or across the docks—is not one soon to be forgotten. The ancient town stands high upon its headland, old houses clustering round the great squat tower of the parish church; in the foreground are warehouses and quays, with a forest of cranes and masts and funnels, the Victorian town of West Hartlepool spreading ever farther south and west. St Aidan, first Bishop of Lindisfarne, founded a monastery on the head-

land in 640, and St Hilda became its Abbess in 646, before moving to Whitby to found the great religious house there. The history of the town and port goes back to the 12th century: its charter as a borough was granted by King John in 1200. Town walls and ten defensive towers were built: until 1700 Hartlepool remained the first port of County Durham; then it sank in status, and in the 18th century became little more than a fishing village. West Hartlepool was founded by Ralph Ward Jackson, solicitor, promoter of the West Hartlepool Harbour and Railway Company and M.P. The harbour was opened in 1835, the railway to Stockton in 1841, and a great new town established. But Hartlepool fought fiercely to retain its independence: only in recent years have the two boroughs been united. *St Hilda's*, the ancient parish church, stands magnificent and venerable in a large, old-fashioned churchyard, in the faded surroundings of the old town, close to the sea. The great west tower (c. 1250) is supported by six tremendous buttresses: the long nave of seven bays (c. 1200), with its clustered columns and single-lancet clerestory, is of equal splendour; the east end, which had become ruinous, was excellently rebuilt by W. D. Caröe in 1924. The vista of nave and chancel from the west end is very grand; behind the High Altar is the tomb of Robert Bruce, founder of the church—the Bruce family were lords of the manor from the 11th to the 14th century—and the baluster-shaped font was the gift of George Bowes, Mayor of Hartlepool, in 1728. South-west of the church stands a fragment of the mediaeval *town wall* and the *Sandwell Gate*; and all around little streets of unassuming Georgian houses and early 19th-century cottages lead to the front. Standing here, above the sea, Old Hartlepool has some of the character of a north-country Kemp Town. Even

St Hilda's, **Hartlepool**

run-down and shabby, the place has undoubted atmosphere—and from the churchyard there is a great view south across the harbour. Just off the road to West Hartlepool stands in a prominent position the great *church of St Oswald* (by W. S. Hicks, 1904), with its tall west tower, and great clerestoried nave and chancel. The interior is equally magnifical and lavishly furnished. The centre of West Hartlepool is Church Square; here on an island stands *Christ Church*, a monster Victorian church by E. B. Lamb (1856), a building of enormous character with its tall west tower (with even taller single pinnacle), squat flèche at the crossing, tran-

septs and apsidal east end; the interior is oppressive with low heavy-timbered roof. No longer a parish church, the building belongs to the town, and is used for functions. Nearby, the *Municipal Buildings* in a flamboyant Flemish style in brick (1889), the *Methodist chapel* with grand Corinthian portico (1870), the *Grand Hotel* (1889) in red brick and terracotta, friendly and impressive with its French mansard towers (by J. Garry), and the large white *Co-op*, with its classical columns and dome (by L. G. Ekins, 1913) are the most prominent buildings. To the west Victoria Road and Grange Road lead out to prosperous Victorian resi-

dential roads; *St Paul's*, by Hodgson Fowler (1885) is here—with tall red tower and short spire. To the south the dual carriageway leads to *Stranton*, a submerged village, with an ancient parish church, which—with its much-weathered Perpendicular tower—stands between Cameron's Brewery and the Stranton Bottling Works. But Church Street leads east to the docks. Here stands the *statue of Ralph Ward Jackson*, 'Founder of this Town, and first Member of Parliament for the Hartlepools'; there are a few buildings to note, such as the *Shades Hotel* with its Art Nouveau terracotta decoration and ironwork, and the *Royal Hotel* with its severer, simpler, late Georgian façade—and the road disappears underground, under the railway, to the docks. It is a pleasure to make one's way, past the *Customs House* (1844), a dignified pedimented brick building, and the old *Dock Office* (1853) with its stone façade and cupola, to the various docks and quaysides. There is a long curving pier, reminiscent of the Cobb at Lyme Regis, guarding the entrance to the old harbour, where small craft are tied up. From here there is the splendid view across to the old town to the north—and to the mouth of the Tees and the Cleveland Hills to the south.

Haswell [11] The derelict colliery land is now being reclaimed: the village comprises the usual terraces of miners' cottages, and a little red-brick Victorian *church* on a hilltop, with a flèche (1870). Across the fields from the main road to Easington stands what appears to be the fragment of a mediaeval building—or perhaps a Roman arch. In fact it is all that remains of the colliery winding tower: as a folly, or reminder of a great local industry, it is splendid and eloquent.

Haughton-le-Skerne [16] A suburb of Darlington, but preserving its long green, bordered by a number of dignified Georgian houses. Norman church with sturdy west tower and 19th-century transepts—and an interior filled with 'Cosin'-type furnishings: box pews with poppyheads and doors, and on either side of the Norman chancel arch a matching pair of pulpit and lectern, with elaborate carved backs and canopies. Rare Royal Arms of George II, erroneously displaying the quarterings of the Stuarts: comparable to the contemporary Royal Arms at Loxhore in Devon, which perpetrates the same heraldic howler.

Haverton Hill [17] A great power station (by Sir Giles Gilbert Scott, 1953) close to the Tees; the ship-

Royal Arms in **Haughton-le-Skerne** church

yard and its offices; otherwise there is little but derelict sites: a few terraces of semi-derelict houses, some with vegetation sprouting from the roof, and the Wellington public house. The road west leads to Billingham, the road east to Port Clarence, the road north to the site of Bellasis (from which the mediaeval family took its name)—and, in semi-rural settings everywhere chemical works, chemical works, chemical works.

Hawthorn [11] The old A19 from Seaham to Easington and the new dual carriageway alongside race by, leaving an unexpected rural oasis here along the coast—one of the last undisfigured stretches of coastline in the Bishoprick. Hawthorn is indeed a small country village, with its little church, its green, and its cottages.

The *church* is a pretty little Victorian building of 1865 with bellcote, and monuments to the family of Pemberton of Hawthorn Tower. Until thirty years ago Hawthorn Tower stood, embowered in trees, on the cliffs above the sea, castellated, pinnacled, romantic—an early 19th-century seaside folly. All that remains is a single solitary look-out tower, away in the fields to the north of the lane that leads to the sea.

Headlam [16] In the by-roads of the delectable countryside north of the Tees, a little hamlet of old farm buildings and stone walls accompanying *Headlam Hall*, one of the best of the many good manor houses to be found in these parts. The west front—facing iron gates and a garden surrounded by low stone walls—appears 18th century,

121

Haughton-le-Skerne church

for the shipbuilder, Andrew Leslie, by Johnson of Newcastle (1872), with its tall, tapering spire, and long, gabled school-building alongside. But much of the square is a car park, a dull terrace on one side, a shipyard and its offices on the other. The air is filled with the hum of industry. St Cuthbert's parish church, round the corner, is unexpectedly modest; nearby, the Caledonian Hotel with its glazed bricks and tiles stands amid wide derelict sites, and towards Jarrow is St Oswald's (1881), a rather more imposing red-brick church in another spreading vacant scene. The only historic building is *Hebburn Hall*, once the seat of the coal-owning Ellisons, its late 18th-century façades concealing an older house, with (perhaps) the masonry of the original pele tower on its west side. The house is now a Masonic Club. Almost attached to the back of the house, and in an odd position, stands *St John's church* with its west bellcote and central flêche, apparently formed out of the stables of the Hall (by M. T. Wilson, 1885). The (ritually) west transept is a kind of ante-chapel: long, aisleless nave and chancel with ornamental roof—the choir fitted out with a forest of carved stalls and canopies in pitch pine. The Hall is approached by an arch at the end of a dull street, south of the main road; at the crossroads opposite, the Headquarters of the Protestant Conservative Club.

with its three floors of long sash windows, its Classical front door and hipped roof: the south front, facing a wide lawn, is similar. Yet its rugged simplicity betrays a Jacobean house, refronted in the 18th century, and it is no surprise to find an earlier façade with mullioned windows at the back. The Headlam family, of distinguished scholars, knights and churchmen (see Whorlton) take their name from here, but Headlam itself passed out of the family by marriage in the 16th century, and the place has passed through many hands since then. There are wide prospects of the Yorkshire hills, across the valley of the Tees.

Hebburn-on-Tyne [4] Shipbuilding. The long, endless, built-up main road from Gateshead to South Shields runs parallel with the river: the cranes of the shipyards are prominent by the waterside, and mean streets lead down to vantage points for watching the great hulks of the boats in building. There is not very much to see in Hebburn: a wide square is dominated by the unexpectedly impressive *St Andrew's Presbyterian church* (now United Reform), built

Heighington [16] Wide, sloping village greens: cottages and terrace houses form an attractive ensemble, with one or two larger houses such as *Heighington Hall* (north-east of the church) with its pronounced stone details, early 18th century. The *church* stands in the middle, and divides green from green. Norman west tower; 13th-century south aisle, 19th-century north aisle. Norman chancel arch, and long chancel with narrower sanctuary. Early 16th-century carved

Headlam Hall and outbuildings

wooden pulpit, with inscription 'Orate pro animabus Alexandri Fletcher et Agnetis uxoris suae'. 16th-century choir stalls, and Victorian box pew of the Surtees of Redworth Hall. Crude painted and carved heraldic monument to George Crosyer (1691); 17th-century brass (chancel wall) to Anthony Byerley of Middridge Grange, the Cavalier; marble monument (sanctuary) to Captain William Cumby, R.N. (1837). 'Captain Superintendent of the

123

Holmside New Hall

Royal Arsenal', reads the inscription, 'and in command of the Royal Sovereign Yacht at the Battle of Trafalgar, where at an early period of the engagement he succeeded to the command of the Bellerophon of 74 guns, which was then opposed in the hottest of the action to a superior force.' Early 17th-century hatchments to the Jennisons of Walworth Castle. *Trafalgar House*, the home of Captain Cumby—and where his descendants still live—is an early 19th-century house, with older outbuildings and stables, standing behind high walls along the road to Aycliffe. *Redworth Hall* is a mile to the north of the village, a

part 16th-century, part 19th-century gabled stone house; it was acquired through marriage with the Croziers (Crosyers) by the Surtees family in the early 18th century—and they greatly enlarged it in the 19th. It is now a county council school. And a mile beyond, remote across the fields, is Middridge Grange, now a gabled farmhouse, but in the 17th century the home of Colonel Anthony Byerley, the Cavalier.

Herrington [5] Colliery country: Shiney Row, Philadelphia, Penshaw, Houghton-le-Spring—the growth is continuous. But near the

Victorian church (1884) are old stone walls and old stone buildings that once surrounded the mansion house of the Ayton family (*see* Washington and Houghton-le-Spring); an unexpected rural oasis.

Hett [10] Turn off the old North Road by the little Victorian church at Croxdale: the lane turns sharply and climbs the hill, passes a tall gabled house with an unexpected little battlemented gazebo on its garden wall—and across a field gate is a distant glimpse of the Orangery of Croxdale Hall. A little way on is the wide village green of Hett: a few cottages, a few newer

124

Horden Hall

houses. The road continues, twists and turns again, to rejoin the main road a mile or so on.

Hetton-le-Hole [11] The Hettons proliferate. There is Hetton-le-Hole, and Hetton-le-Hill. To the south-east is South Hetton, and to the south-west is (mysteriously enough) East Hetton. Coal dominates them all. It was here that, in the early 19th century, the deep East Durham coalfield was first developed. The Hetton Coal Company raised its first coal from under the deep limestone band in 1822—after twelve years of sinking—and the company established itself as the great rival of the Lambtons and the Londonderrys. The extensive mines at East Rainton nearby belonged to Londonderry, and at one stage he tried to buy the Hetton Company—but failed. The newly established railway to Sunderland in the 1820s provided a ready outlet for Hetton coal, and an increased impetus to the company. Londonderry's reply was the construction of the harbour at Seaham, for his coal. There is a *church* of blackened stone (1843) in the main street; more prominent from a distance, and standing boldly above the houses, is the red-brick church of *Eppleton* (1883)—but it is not easy to approach: a labyrinth of council houses stands between it and the main road, and the would-be visitor may never reach its door. Beyond the council houses slag heaps loom. To the south-east is the village of *Lyons*, with a characteristic church of 1869 on the main road. The strange name of the place is due to John Lyon of Hetton House, grandson of the 8th Earl of Strathmore—who had married a local heiress. In 1810 he decided to explore for coal. He explored for ten years, sank shafts of 120 feet, spent £13,000—and found no coal! Poor Mr Lyon went bankrupt; the Hetton Company took over, and two years later reached the coal. But the name of John Lyon lives on.

Heworth [4] Between Felling and Hebburn, one mass of industry and Victorian housing close to the Tyne: the church and the Hall and the Swan Inn stand at the intersection of the A184 and A185—the traffic swirls by, with the railway in a cutting below. The *church* is of

125

1822, designed by the rector John Hodgson and the architect John Stokoe, and has a bold pinnacled west tower, aisleless nave, chancel and transepts in the thin Gothic of the period. In the churchyard is the tomb of the Haddon children, lying under a stone four-poster with pillows and bedspread (1717). The *Hall* (now the Conservative Club) is a good-looking 18th-century stone house, standing incongruously above the railway cutting. The A185 leads on to Hebburn—the road opposite up to Felling.

High Coniscliffe *see* Coniscliffe, High

High Etherley *see* Etherley, High

High Spen *see* Spen, High

Hollinside [9] (near Lanchester) Two miles south-west of Lanchester on the road to Wolsingham is a long terrace of Gothick cottages, with Gothick windows and pretty glazing bars; *Hollinside Hall* nearby is a plain Victorian classical house, commanding the wide view to the east.

Hollinside Hall or **Old Hollinside** [4] (near Gibside) In a beautiful position above the River Derwent stand the ruins of Hollinside, a mediaeval fortified manor house, with Great Hall, approached by a gatehouse, and a smaller tower closer to the river. Held by the Redheughs and afterwards by a family called de Outhe, it passed by marriage to the Hardinges (of the distinguished military and naval family)—the last of whom, 'pressed by many misfortunes', sold it to George Bowes of Gibside in 1730, since when it has become a romantic ruin.

Holmside [4] The bleak road to the moors north-east of Lanchester passes old pits and collieries, new opencast mines, and *Burnhope church* (1865—one long nave and chancel,

with little half-shafts dividing nave and chancel with a wooden chancel arch); Holmside is merely a small collection of cottages. But up a narrow lane is an old farmhouse called *Holmside Hall*, which incorporates in its farm buildings a few remains of the mediaeval manor house of the Tempests (*see also* Stella and Wynyard). On the windswept hillside half a mile to the south-west is *Holmside New Hall*, which should be visited before it crumbles away. 'Timo Whittingham hanc domum edificabat anno 1668 et illam non indigne vocabat Little Homside', reads the inscription over the front door. It is a simple three-storeyed stone façade with mullioned windows. But if it is possible to make one's way through the nettles round to the east side there is an entirely different early 18th-century front of two storeys, with sash windows and an imposing pedimented doorway. The windows are broken, the roof is collapsing; however it is just possible to discern fragments of panelling within. There are a few derelict farm buildings around, and one (inhabited) cottage. That is all. A beautiful, moving, melancholy relic.

Horden [11] The road east from Peterlee descends to the sea, to Horden. There is terrace upon terrace of miners' cottages, built to house the men working in the great collieries along the coast—and an imposing cruciform *church* with low central tower built in 1913 by the Burdons of Castle Eden; stone outside, brick and stone within, this is a building with handsome furnishings, and powerful Anglo-Catholic atmosphere. Along the coast road (A1086), a little further north, the road divides—and a narrow farm lane leads steeply down to *Horden Hall*, from the high road an astonishing sight—the perfect small Jacobean manor house, enclosed in a walled garden; new council estates over its shoulder on one

side, rough farmland and the sea on the other. The house was built c. 1600 by Sir Christopher Conyers (of the Sockburn family, q.v.): there are two main storeys with a steeply pitched roof above a shallow attic floor, and pairs of large mullioned windows on either side of the porch. This, with its coupled Tuscan columns, its sophisticated carving, its quartered coat of arms above the door, supporting a seven-light bay window on the first floor, makes an imposing centrepiece. After the death of Sir Baldwin Conyers in 1767 the place was sold to the Burdons of Castle Eden: elaborate panelling was subsequently moved to their new house there, and the splendid staircase is now in the Bowes Museum. Horden descended to farmhouse status, and stands now, accompanied by old farm buildings, beautiful and a little forlorn in these strange new surroundings.

Houghton-le-Spring [5] (pronounced Hoton) On the main road from Durham to Sunderland (A690): the new dual carriageway cuts savagely through the town, and there is the usual accompaniment of roundabouts and new approach roads. But Houghton itself is ancient, and until the development of the East Durham coalfield in the early 19th century was a quiet market town. There are still some relics of its antiquity. First, the important *parish church*: there is one Norman window, and the small Norman door into the sacristy nearby (with its tympanum of fighting animals), in the north wall of the chancel, to remind us of the earliest church; in the south wall of the chancel is a line of eight little Early English lancet windows of considerable beauty; but the general impression is of a church of the Decorated period, with notable traceried windows at the east and west ends and in the south transept. The church indeed is cruciform and spacious, with

Helmington Hall, **Hunwick**

bold central tower (the upper part is of 1823, taking the place of the thin lead spire that appears in old pictures). There is a distinguished late 15th-century two-storeyed chantry on the south side of the chancel, which was formerly detached. Houghton was in the past an extremely well-endowed living, and many eminent men have held it, including two who later became Archbishops of Canterbury. But the greatest name among them is that of Bernard Gilpin, 'the Apostle of the North'. Born in 1517, the nephew of Bishop Tunstall, Gilpin became rector here in 1558. Brought up and ordained in the pre-Reformation Church, he continued to say the old Latin Mass, 'but seldom and privately', and was a devout sacramentalist; yet with his study of the Bible and the Fathers he was no longer able to uphold the supremacy of the Pope or the truth of some Roman doctrines. He was a man of sweet reasonableness in turbulent and troublous times, and the forerunner of those saintly and scholarly divines who have been the glory of the Church of England. Although offered the Bishopric of Carlisle, he preferred to remain Rector of Houghton, where he died in 1583. Gilpin used the great endowments of the living to the glory of God and in the service of his fellow men, keeping open house in the Rectory, and providing dinner on Sundays to all who came: at his table one might meet the great Lord Burghley or any of the twenty-four poor men whom he fed weekly at his own expense. He founded the grammar school, and himself boarded and taught many of its pupils in his own house. His generosity, and his self-effacement, became legendary. Gilpin's tomb stands prominent in the south transept; nearby is the brass of Margery Bellasis (1587), a friend of Gilpin's, a pious widow and mother

127

Hunstanworth church

of twelve. Opposite are the marble tablets to Sir Francis Blake, Bt, F.R.S., of Twizel, the mathematician (1780), and to his wife Isabel, daughter of Samuel Ayton 'of West Herrington in this parish, descended of an Honourable and Ancient family'. At the east end of the church stands the old *Kepier Grammar School*, founded by Gilpin and his friend John Heath, who gave the endowments from the old Kepier Hospital at Durham (q.v.)—now used as parish hall. And nearby are the *Davenport Alms-houses*, founded by a 17th-century rector, George Davenport. At the west end of the church is the great *rectory* (now council offices): partly mediaeval, the house was much rebuilt in the 17th century, and

remodelled in the 18th; its garden is a public park. The new dual carriageway has cut off Church Street from the pleasant 18th-century terraces that still stand on the other side of the traffic-filled abyss; and from the *Old Hall*, a great square three-storeyed Elizabethan building, now used as a club. A vast council estate spreads to the south. Warden Law, the hill north of the town, is much scarred by mining.

Howden-le-Wear [10] Travelling from Witton-le-Wear Howden appears in a pretty setting in the green valley of the Beechburn Beck. The village grew in the 19th century round the (now extinct) colliery, and modern industry stretches up the hill north to Crook.

Little *church* (1862) with nave and chancel, bellcote and lancet windows, in a back street. The railway from Bishop Auckland to Crook and Tow Law is also now extinct.

Hunstanworth [2] Glorious remote moorland country, where the River Derwent divides County Durham from Northumberland: woodlands of larch and oak conceal the few signs of habitation. A bridge leads across to Blanchland, a foot into Northumberland, but redolent of Durham, for the whole idyllic village, built in the 18th century within the walls of a dissolved Premonstratensian abbey, belongs to the Crewe Trustees, and in the dining room of the Lord Crewe Arms hang portraits of that great

128

18th-century Bishop of Durham, Nathaniel Lord Crewe, and his wife Dorothy Forster. The village of Hunstanworth is quite different, but also unusual. Church, vicarage, school, and every house and cottage, were built by a Victorian squarson, the Revd D. Capper, and he chose for his architect S. S. Teulon. Teulon, with his love of varied textures and colours, designed every building of contrasting stone and varied tiles and slates, and his Gothic gabled cottages are highly picturesque. The *Church* (1865) is quite unnecessarily commodious for so small a village, with spacious nave and north aisle, apsidal chancel and solid northeast tower with pyramid roof. The interior is equally decorative: the pulpit emerges from an arcaded recess on the south, and the walls are adorned with florid painted texts.

Hunwick [10]

In the grimmest decayed industrial countryside between Crook and Bishop Auckland—the railway uprooted, the whole landscape one of miserable broken-down industry. There is a *church* of 1844 (by W. Thompson) which was enlarged in 1877—a building with rows of lancet windows, and rows of pitch pine pews, the interior aglow with gaudy Victorian stained glass. But *Hunwick Old Hall* is a mediaeval manor house, long since sunk to farmhouse status; there is a half-hexagon bay window on the front, and the former chapel, now a barn, still retains its traceried east window—remarkable relics which have only survived by neglect. On the green outside the gate is a 'gin' or engine house for horse-powered machinery. North of the village, *Helmington Hall* is the fragment (now a farm) of a much larger house of 1686: a few pedimented sash windows survive.

Hurworth [16]

Croft Bridge is the frontier post between County Durham and the North Riding: Croft, with its Spa Hotel and ancient church, is in Yorkshire—but the church contains that most spectacular family pew of the Milbankes of Halnaby, which stands on columns above the nave, like a private box at an opera house—and the Milbankes were closely connected with County Durham (*see* Seaham and Washington). *Croft Bridge*, probably built by Bishop Skirlaw in the early 14th century, has been widened over the centuries, and carries the old Great North Road on seven ribbed arches. It was for centuries the scene of the ceremonial entry of the Prince Bishops to the diocese (*see* Neasham). A mile downstream the railway bridge (1840) carries the London to Edinburgh line across the river. Hurworth with its long village green lies on the north bank; on either side of the long street are cottages and larger houses facing the green—notably the bay-windowed manor house (1728), now a preparatory school. The *church* stands on a cliff above the river: 15th-century tower, the rest largely rebuilt by J. P. Pritchett in 1870, but incorporating fragments of the earlier building, and containing two 14th-century tombs of knights from Neasham. In the churchyard is the tomb of William Emerson, eccentric mathematical genius (d. 1782), with epitaphs in Hebrew and Latin.

Hutton Henry [11]

Just off the A19—the high road from Sunderland to Stockton—and set back from the side road and partly screened by trees, stands *Hutton House*, a red-brick house of 1825 with shallow bow windows. Attached to it is an ecclesiastical-looking building in brighter red brick. What is this? It is the Roman Catholic chapel and presbytery of SS. Peter and Paul. In this isolated spot in 1825 the last Roman Catholic chaplain at Hardwick Hall (*see* Blackhall) bought land and built a small chapel and priest's house: after 250 years at Hardwick the Maire family were selling up. So the chapel at Hutton inherited the parish at Hardwick. A new, larger chapel was built in 1895: it is a pretty little basilica, with apsidal east end. Further up the lane is the village: a little green-lined street climbing the hill, with a small red-brick Victorian aisleless *church* on the right.

Hutton Magna [15]

An entrancing spot, in the magnificent wide landscape of the North Riding—now annexed by County Durham. A village street of low cottages and pretty gardens and trees: next to the public house is the entrance to the churchyard, half hidden and mysterious. The *church* was rebuilt in 1878 by Austin, Johnson and Hicks, and with its fragments from the earlier church, its bellcote and its scholarly details is a comely little building. Glorious views across churchyard to the west, where the Hall, a Tudor gabled H-shaped house with mullioned and later sash windows stands among old farm buildings in the meadows. The R.C. church of Wycliffe is a more distant landmark on the higher ground to the north.

Hylton Castle [5]

Lost in the west suburbs of Sunderland: a wide lawn, a grove of trees—all else is a sea of new houses. But it stands close to the B1289 (Sunderland to Washington), and the exploring traveller may yet discover it. Built in the early 15th century by the Hylton family, who took their name and title from the place, it stands tall and solid with four square turrets on the west side, a low wide tower above the battlements on the east. Hyltons remained in possession until the early 18th century, when the heiress married Sir Richard Musgrave of Hayton Castle, Cumberland. Their daughter married William Jolliffe, M.P., whose grandson was created

Lord Hylton, of Ammerdown, Somerset. Hylton was acquired by the Bowes family, and was last inhabited early this century. In the 18th century wings were added to north and south, charmingly crenellated—and handsome pedimented sash windows inserted, with a Strawberry Hill Gothick porch; the house never looked more delightful (see the drawing in Robert Billings, *Architectural Antiquities of County Durham*, 1846). But in a purist restoration in 1869 the wings were pulled down, and 'mediaeval' windows replaced. The poor house now appears somewhat sad and sombre. The ruins of the 15th-century chapel stand behind, with Tudor bay windows added in the 16th century, and a Classical doorway in the 18th. The castle is now in the care of the Department of the Environment.

Ingleton [10] Small village in the pleasant open country north of the Tees, on the minor road (B6279) between Darlington and Staindrop. Simple little Victorian *church* by Bonomi and Cory (1844) by the roadside.

Jarrow [4] Durham of Durham of Durham: the remarkable juxtaposition of 19th-century industry and ancient English history. The 19th-century town lies to the west: there is the Victorian *town hall*, and the church of *Christ Church*, Jarrow Grange (1868), with its tall broach spire, its tower distinguished by tall lancets and little round windows above. Drab streets lead down to the river with its shipyards. Close to Christ Church is the *statue of Sir Charles Mark Palmer*, founder of the shipyards, M.P. for North Durham and for Jarrow (d. 1907). The shipyards closed in 1934: the depression and the hunger marches followed, and a plaque at the entrance to the town hall recalls the events of those days. Now few remember them: great tower blocks of flats rise above the wasteland of demolished streets; dual carriageways, round-

abouts and underpasses connect the new motorway to the Tyne Tunnel or the A19 to Middlesbrough and the south, and the traffic rushes on its way. New industries have been established and new wealth created—and a new shopping-centre serves as its symbol. There is a Victorian *R.C. church* dedicated to St Bede, with elaborate traceried windows and prominent pinnacles. A signpost 'ST PAUL'S MONASTERY' at the roundabout leads to the celebrated church and monastic ruins where Bede lived and wrote his *Ecclesiastical History* (A.D. 731). Jarrow Slake is still a derelict swamp, as it was in Bede's time: there are views down river to South Shields—but oil and petrol storage tanks crown the low hill to the north: timber yards and the Bede Trading Estate are hard by. *Jarrow Hall*, the late Georgian villa across the greensward, serves as a modern *hospitium* for today's pilgrims, and contains refreshment rooms and a local museum. The *church* itself has a spacious nave and north aisle by Sir Gilbert Scott (1866), built to replace a Norman nave destroyed in 1786. The chancel is the nave of the Saxon church: between the Victorian nave and this Saxon chancel stands the venerable Norman tower (c. 1075). The dedication stone recalling the foundation of the church and monastery in 684 miraculously survives, as does an ancient chair, said to be Bede's but in reality (probably) 14th century. Much excavation has been carried out in recent years, and impressive walls of the monastic house stand to the south of the church—part Saxon, part 11th-century—and it is easy to imagine Bede coming here at the age of 12, and here devoting his life to his *History* and to his *Commentaries*. Here he died on the Eve of the Ascension, 735.

Kelloe [11] Scarred countryside of the old coalfield south-east of Durham: terraces of miners' cot-

tages, newer council houses, a public house called the Davy Lamp. To the north of the village a road leads across a level crossing without gates (the track leads to the pit) to the *church*, set in sudden rural surroundings in the greenest of green valleys. A small Norman building, dedicated to St Helen, with west tower heavily buttressed on the south side, and Early English chancel with small lancets and later traceried windows, the church is famed for the Kelloe Cross, one of the most notable of all Norman crosses. The cross head is remarkably well preserved: on the broad shaft below are three tiers of sculptured figures: at the top St Helena is seen entranced, receiving the vision in which she was instructed to find the Holy Cross; below, the saint appears with a companion, and at the bottom she is seen menacing Judas Iscariot with a sword, and ordering him to dig with his spade to uncover the cross. Of great interest, too, is the tablet commemorating 'the birth in this parish of Elizabeth Barrett Browning ... a great poetess, a noble woman, a devoted wife'. She was born in 1806 at Coxhoe Hall (q.v.), then in this parish. Coxhoe and Kelloe seem a far cry from Rome and Florence where she and Robert Browning chiefly lived.

Kirk Merrington [10] On the high ground south of Spennymoor: the church tower is a landmark for miles around. Old Collieries and their attendant clutter are scattered about. The *church* is a rebuilding (1850) of one of the finest Norman churches in the county: old prints show the original building; the reproduction, with its 19th-century features, is correct but a trifle hard. With central tower, aisleless nave and chancel, the church has, however, a certain magnificence. 17th-century 'Cosin' screen. In a well-wooded park to the south stands *Windlestone Hall*, the former great house of the Eden family. Built in

Kelloe church

1834 by Bonomi to replace an earlier house, it stands long and two-storeyed, with top balustrade and, on the ground floor, a long colonnade of coupled Tuscan columns, the whole faced with banded rustication such as Bonomi loved to use. The stables have a tower crowned with a large open cupola, a little reminiscent of Wallington. Handsome little lodge on main road with temple front. Sir Timothy Eden writes movingly of Windlestone in his *Tribulations of a Baronet*, and of his father Sir William, the Victorian painter. Windlestone was sold by the family in 1936, and the house is now a county council school. The Eden Arms, so prominent on the old Great North Road at Rushyford, keeps their great name alive. (*See also* West Auckland.)

Lambton [4] 'No earlier owners of Lambton are on record than the ancient and honourable family which still bears the local name', wrote Surtees; and 150 years later the Lambton family, Earls of Durham, are still in possession, Lambton itself being an incredible oasis, hemmed in between Chester-le-Street and Shiney Row, between railways and dual carriageways, almost overtaken by industry. But an oasis of astonishing beauty it remains. A little north of Chester-le-Street, close to the A1 (M), the River Wear is spanned by the 15th-century *Bridgeford Bridge*, with a Classical arch by Ignatius Bonomi (1815) at the far end. This is the private entrance to Lambton Park, which covers some 2,000 acres and extends along steep wooded banks on both sides of the

132

Kelloe Cross ▷
(*and opposite*)

Ravensworth (*see* **Lamesley**)

river. The scene has changed but little since John Glover painted his pictures of Lambton for the 1st Earl (c. 1830): there is the first sight of the castle from the Lamb Bridge (by Ignatius Bonomi, 1820), and a little further on the castle stands directly above the river, surveying the wooded bank opposite—the trees reflected in the dark water in between. It is the perfect creation of the early 19th-century 'romantic landscape', the castle itself built originally by Bonomi between 1820 and 1828. The original Lambton Hall was further on to the east. This was the scene of the old legend of the Lambton worm—a relation, no doubt, of the Sockburn worm—which was caught unwittingly by the young heir to Lambton, who was fishing in the Wear one Sunday morning when he should have been in church. The terrible serpent (or dragon), though promptly deposited in a local well, grew in size and awesomeness, became in time

a terror to the neighbourhood and ravaged the district. Some years later the young heir, having repented of his ways and gone on a Crusade, returned home—and consulted a sibyl. He could only destroy the worm, she told him, by protecting himself with armour studded with razor blades; he should slay it on its rock in mid-stream, where the current would carry off its severed parts, and so avoid the danger of their being reunited. In return he must vow he would slay the next living creature he encountered, 'or the lords of Lambton would not die in their beds for nine generations'. The worm was duly slain, but on hearing the sound of victory the old father forgot to unleash a favourite hound as the promised sacrifice, and ran to embrace his son. The hound was duly sacrificed—but too late; and for nine generations no Lambton died in his bed. At the end of the 17th century Ralph

Lambton married the heiress of the Hedworth family of Harraton Hall, a house which stood not far from Lambton, but on a finer site. This is the house which, now encased in Gothic dress, enlarged and glorified, is *Lambton Castle*. Between 1820 and 1828 Bonomi encased the old Harraton, gothicized it, crenellated it, enlarged it: flying buttresses on the south front conceal the old house, of which one or two early 18th-century rooms survive behind. The *Flag Tower*, another tower, a long terrace, fortifications—all were added, and the transformation was complete. Unfortunately, owing to mining subsidence, the house nearly collapsed thirty years later; in the 1860s John Dobson and Sidney Smirke (his son-in-law) were called in to rebuild and enlarge; but much of what they added was pulled down in 1930. For some years the castle was used as a teacher training college; now the park has

134

become a nature reserve, and is open to the public. Lord Lambton lives at *Biddick Hall*, an interesting and most handsome house, on the edge of the park, to the east. It is a grand house in miniature: its south front, of warm red brick, approached by an ancient avenue, is five bays wide, with long sash windows on two floors, with giant Ionic pilasters marking the centre, and urns crowning the parapet and central pediment. Biddick was bought in the early 17th century by Sir William Lambton, who was slain at Marston Moor, for his younger son. An earlier house, or pele tower, stood on the site, and is encased in the bones of the present house which was built by Freville Lambton c. 1720. The house has about it a Vanbrugian air, and the baroque plaster ceiling to the staircase bears a distinct resemblance to that in the Garter Room at Lumley. So it is possible that Vanbrugh may have had some hand in Biddick—but a stone's throw from the Lumley cousins. The Lambtons have always been a fiercely independent race, untitled aristocrats until the 1st Lord Durham accepted a barony in 1828. An early Lambton was Master of Balliol, another Knight of Rhodes; Sir William (killed at Marston Moor) commanded the Durham Dragoons for Charles I. His great grandson, General John Lambton, M.P. for Durham, declined a peerage in 1793, and his grandson, William Henry, M.P., continued the parliamentary tradition and was a brilliant Whig, friend of Lord Grey, of Samuel Whitbread and of Fox. John George Lambton, 1st Earl of Durham (1833), one of the most eminent sons of the county, was his son. Nicknamed Radical Jack, and King Jog ('jogging along on £40,000 a year'), he married the daughter of Lord Grey, Prime Minister at the time of the Reform Bill; Cabinet Minister and Lord Privy Seal, he was one of the committee of four who drafted the Bill. But for professional jealousy, he might have become Prime Minister: instead he became Ambassador to St Petersburg (1834), and in 1838 Governor-General of Canada. It was his celebrated *Durham Report* that laid the foundations of the British Empire, and Canada became the first self-governing Dominion of the Commonwealth. He died in 1840 at the age of 48, a much-loved public hero in the north of England, especially among the miners of County Durham, for whom he established a Benevolent Association for old and sick miners in his collieries. The Penshaw Monument (q.v.) is his memorial.

Lamesley [4] The *church* looks like a church in Kent, mysteriously transplanted—with its tower with staircase turret. But here it stands in strange isolation, the main railway line to Newcastle with its great attendant sidings to the east, and the road to the Team Valley Trading Estate to the north. There is little village—a huddle of cottages and an inn away to the west, and, over the hill, the colliery village of Kibblesworth. In fact the church is of 1821, in neo-Perpendicular, with an elegant galleried interior which recalls a church in London. In the chancel are a number of 19th-century monuments to the Liddells of Ravensworth Castle. The demesne of *Ravensworth*, wooded and secluded for all the proximity of Team Valley, lies on rising ground to the north-west. A few fragments of the mediaeval castle of the FitzMarmadukes survive: the property was purchased in 1607 by Thomas Liddell, a prosperous Alderman of Newcastle, whose grandson was created a baronet by Charles I, in recognition of his defence of Newcastle against the Scots in 1642. The family prospered exceedingly on coal, and in turn became Barons and Earls of Ravensworth. The mediaeval castle was replaced by a house of 1724; and Sir Thomas Liddell, later 1st Lord Ravensworth, commissioned John Nash to build the new castle in 1808. Embattled and turreted, with a gatehouse and surrounding towers, a Great Hall and grand staircase, saloon and conservatory, Ravensworth was the epitome of Nash's romantic Gothic palaces. The 1st Lord Ravensworth was a great coal magnate, friend and patron of George Stephenson, friend of the Duke of Wellington—who paid a visit to the castle in 1820. His nephew was Henry George Liddell, Dean of Christ Church and Vice Chancellor of Oxford, immortalized in Liddell and Scott's Greek *Lexicon*, whose daughter Alice was the Alice of *Alice in Wonderland*, written for her amusement by the Revd C. L. Dodgson (Lewis Carroll), her parents' friend and neighbour. Nash's castle was demolished in 1953; the stableyard and gatehouse survive, with one of Nash's towers, forming an effective quasi-mediaeval ruin, with two genuine mediaeval towers and some curtain walling. At the point where two drives meet stands the mediaeval Butter Cross; the estate still belongs to Lord Ravensworth, and is not open to the public.

Lanchester [9, 10] Longovicium, the long fort of the Roman occupation: the Roman camp was half a mile south of the village, on the high ground close to the road to Wolsingham. There is very little above ground—the stone from the fort has over the centuries been used for local buildings—but in the 2nd and 3rd centuries A.D this was a place of great importance, on the road from York to Hadrian's Wall. The village now surrounds a wide-spreading green at the point where four major roads—from Durham, from Stanley, from Wolsingham and from Consett—meet: it is good, hilly, well-wooded country. The tall tower of the *church* faces the green. This is Perpendicular

135

Lanchester

—elegant and embattled with a pretty weather-vane on the south-west pinnacle. Externally, with its long, embattled, clerestoried nave and embattled aisles, the church looks all Perpendicular: it is only on entering that its true Norman and Early English character is discerned. There is a grand Norman chancel arch; the nave of four bays is Transitional, and the cylindrical piers are Roman monoliths from the fort. The chancel is Early English, with lancet windows at the east end and important cusped door to the vestry (north side) with carved tympanum of Our Lord and two attendant angels—the central figure somewhat battered. The carved-head corbels for candles are also interesting and rare. Towards the end of the 13th century the

church was raised to collegiate status, with Dean and Canons, for whom the chancel was fitted up with the stalls and misericords. There is some 13th-century glass in the chancel, and some 15th-century heraldic glass (Tempest family—*see* Holmside) in the south aisle. Over the tower arch is a very fine Royal Arms (George III, 1767) and a gaily painted clock face. There are several monuments worth noting, including the tablet (1794) to George Clavering of Greencroft Hall (son of Sir John Clavering of Axwell, *see* Blaydon), with his hatchment; and one to William Hedley of Burnhopeside Hall, the railway pioneer who designed 'Wylam Dilly' in 1814; and a pretty Gothick tablet (with urns) to Ralph Pemberton (1841).

There are good modern oak pews, and a complete list of 'Rectors, Deans, Perpetual Curates, Intruders and Titular Vicars'. And in the south porch is a Roman altar to the goddess Garmangabis, which (according to the inscription) was erected at the Fort in A.D. 244. Most of the village lies south-west of the green: the street leads to the 1930s basilica-type *R.C. church* in its pretty garden setting. *Greencroft Hall* was a late 17th-century house lying deeply sequestered in woods to the north-west—it was demolished a few years ago. *Greenwell Ford*, south of the village, has been the home of the Greenwell family since 1633; the best-known member of the family was the Revd William Greenwell, D.C.L., F.R.S., the great Durham

△ High Force from above...

◁ ...from below (*see* **Langdon Beck**)

archaeologist. *Burnhopeside* is a neat 19th-century Grecian villa-type house, now hotel, lying on south side of the road to Durham.

Langdon Beck [8] Loneliest of lonely country in the Upper Upper Tees: the road from here across Langdon Fell to St John's Chapel ranks as the highest classified road in England (2,056 feet). There is the Langdon Beck Hotel, a youth hostel, and a small *church* (the parish of Forest and Frith) built in 1875—which looks almost like an outcrop of stone in this landscape of bleak moorland. Life here is so lonely in winter that a previous incumbent remarked to a chance visitor that he and his wife were pleased even by the milkman's

occasional call, so rare were the visits of any friends. A little to the south the River Tees makes it way through scenery of great grandeur to that series of dramatic waterfalls, Cauldron Snout, High Force and Low Force, between here and Middleton-in-Teesdale. *Cauldron Snout* is a long cascade of rushing, bubbling water, just below the new Cow Green Reservoir. It can only be reached by a wild track across Widdybank Fell: beyond the reservoir Cumberland, Westmorland and County Durham meet. *High Force* is a few miles downstream, on the frontier of Durham and York-shire, and is more easily accessible, from the B6277. The High Force Hotel is on the road; at its side is surely one of the best-designed car

parks in England: banks of grass and newly planted trees and shrubs soften the allotted spaces for the regiment of cars. Opposite the hotel a walk through thick woods, frag-rant with garlic in early summer, leads along the steep bank—and then the distant roar of rushing water can be heard. High Force is the highest waterfall in England (70 feet): between great rocks the waters of the infant Tees roar in almighty spate into a cauldron pool below. *Low Force*, less dramatic, is close to Newbiggin, where the river tumbles more gently into Teesdale.

Langley Park [10] Signposts point to Langley Park. A stately home? Open to the public? The road plunges into the drabbest of valleys: run-down collieries, run-down factories, run-down streets of miners' cottages, a run-down Dance Hall (For Sale, 1978), a torn-up railway—only the small church, a little red-brick conventicle, showing signs of life. What was indeed a Park, a mediaeval hunting park in the once-beautiful stretch of country between Durham and Lanchester, was sacrificed to mining and industry in the mid-19th century. Only one thing can be said for this sad little town: the streets are very wide, almost grand—an omen for a renascent town, when industry revives, and prosperity returns?

Lartington [15] The road west from Barnard Castle south of the Tees (B6277) skirts the park, and there are views of the *Hall*, an 18th-century house for centuries the home of the recusant family of Maire, whose monuments are in Romaldkirk Church. The house contains a Georgian Gothick (former) Roman Catholic chapel, with pretty plasterwork and gallery within, which since the extinction of the Maires is used for occasional Anglican services. There is a village street of captivating cottages—and a Victorian R. C. church beyond.

Long Newton *see* Newton, Long

Low Dinsdale *see* Dinsdale, Low

Ludworth [11] (near Shadforth) High exposed country: the small village of an extinct colliery. There is an amusing little Icelandic-looking wooden *church* with a flèche—and along the road to the west the gaunt fragment of *Ludworth Tower* close to the road. Sir Thomas Holden was granted licence by Bishop Langley 'firmare, kirnellare, batillare et tumillare' his manor of Ludworth in 1422: after a century and more of decay, the major portion collapsed in 1890, and it now stands like a broken tooth in this isolated, lonely place.

Ludworth Tower

Lumley, Great [4] A mile or two south of Lumley Castle (*see* Chester-le-Street); a former colliery village—with the usual miners' houses (now being smartened up), and the usual Victorian church (1862).

Medomsley [3] In the high country above the River Derwent: fine views across the river into Northumberland. A scattered village of farms and cottages and many newer houses—surprisingly rural for all the influence of old industry in the district. Distinguished *church*: bellcote and long nave, long chancel and lancet windows—the exterior is one of modest and ancient charm. In fact the nave is a scholarly rebuilding of 1878; the chancel is a perfect example of 13th-century Early English work. Beautiful east end with lancets and stone shafts; on either side two corbel heads as at Lanchester for

carrying lights; oak stalls, oak pews and screen constitute a well-furnished interior. 18th- and 19th-century monuments to the Hunter family, of whom the most notable was General Sir Martin Hunter, Governor of Stirling Castle.

Middleton-in-Teesdale [8] Dour but attractive little town in Upper Teesdale, with two wide streets forming the letter L: many Victorian terraces of stone cottages and larger houses. The village grew in the 19th century with the expansion of the lead industry. *Middleton House* on the hill to the north-west, with its clock-turreted stable, was the headquarters of the London Lead Company; and the *Bainbridge Memorial fountain* (1877) in the middle of the town, with its cast-iron canopy, is a tribute to the manager. The *church* is a rebuilding (1886) by Hodgson Fowler: the interior is well furnished and

The Bainbridge Memorial Fountain, **Middleton-in-Teesdale**

correct. In north-west corner of the churchyard is a little detached 16th-century bell chamber, looking like a rustic garden building. In Town End (east end of the town) is a magnificent Victorian *chapel*, of commanding size and height, with an array of little finials crowning the gable of the entrance front; and, almost opposite, an auspicious-looking archway leads to nothing but some cottages in stone-walled gardens, and so down to the river. A mile or two beyond the town, on the road to Barnard Castle, stands *Stotley Hall*, a 17th-century farmhouse, surrounded by ample buildings. To the west, two miles

upstream, is the *Winch Bridge*, a pedestrian suspension bridge built in 1744 (rebuilt in 1828) for the lead miners—the earliest suspension bridge in Europe. And all around is the grand sweep of lonely landscape—a landscape of sheep and hills and moors.

Middleton St George [17] The humble little *church* of St George stands alone in cornfields, in a high position off the road from Middleton One Row to Aislaby: a low nave and chancel, partly 13th century, partly 18th, with some early 19th-century monuments and a little heraldic glass in the chancel,

and some very odd Victorian pews in the nave—looking like seats on an old railway station. A delectable spot, with wide views across the Tees to Yorkshire. Middleton One Row is in a dramatic position high above the river. The One Row is a long line of early 19th-century houses overlooking the steep grassy bank, down to the river below. It grew up as an appendage to Dinsdale Spa ($\frac{1}{4}$ mile upstream), and is like a humbler version of a terrace at Tunbridge Wells: it is a delightful ensemble, the Devonport Hotel its centrepiece. At the west end, at the corner of the road to Fighting Cocks, stands the Victorian *church of St Laurence* (by J. P. Pritchett, 1871). Teesside Airport is to the north-east, close to the Stockton–Darlington road. At Low Middleton, two miles to the south-east, stands *Low Middleton Hall*, an early 18th-century brick house—with long façade of ten sash windows to the south, and a Victorian Gothic front overlooking the road. The road meanders on to Aislaby and Yarm.

Monk Hesledon [11] Old mining community close to Castle Eden: the disused colliery buildings and winding tower stand gaunt on the edge of the village; there is a public house called the *Golden Calf*, and the *church* is a very-red-brick tabernacle, with a clock in the west gable. The old village, a mere handful of houses, is a mile away at the end of a cul-de-sac. The old church stood across the fields, on the edge of a steep dene—a simple building of 1800, with Gothick windows and box pews. It was, alas, pulled down a few years ago, and now only the overgrown churchyard survives.

Muggleswick [3] Moorland country: here the River Derwent divides Northumberland from County Durham, and there are wide views across a landscape of bracken and sheep. A gated road leads down to a farm and its attendant buildings and cottages, and the little church. And beyond the farm are the unexpected and impressive remains of a great mediaeval *manor house*. It was here that the Priors of Durham had a grange, and the remains comprise an enormous solid stone gable with traceried window and fireplace—probably built by Prior Hugh of Darlington in the 13th century. The little *church* lies across a field behind the farm, a simple affair of 1869, well furnished with modern oak stalls and organ. It is a surprise to turn the corner and see across the sloping churchyard a distant view of the steelworks and smoke of Consett, in all their sombre splendour.

Murton [11] Blackest and bleakest of colliery villages: Hetton-le-Hole, Lyons, Easington Lane, Eppleton, Murton—it is collieries, collieries, collieries, all the way to the coast. Not to be missed for local atmosphere.

Neasham [16] A row of cottages, and a green sward of grass, along the bank of the River Tees, with wide views up and down the river where it makes a graceful bend towards the peninsula of Sockburn. Nothing remains of the abbey, a Benedictine nunnery founded in the reign of Henry II, though the effigies in Hurworth church are supposed to come from here. At Neasham Ford (and later at Croft Bridge) the Prince Bishops of Durham would enter the diocese on their appointment, and be presented with the Conyers falchion by the lord of Sockburn. 'My Lord Bishop', ran the greeting, 'I here present you with the falchion wherewith the champion Conyers slew the worm, dragon or fiery flying serpent which destroyed man, woman and child; in memory of which the king then reigning gave him the manor of Sockburn, to hold by this tenure, that upon the first

entrance of every bishop into the county the falchion should be presented.' The last bishop to receive the falchion was Van Mildert; the falchion may be seen in the museum at the cathedral.

Newbottle [4] An old pottery village, of faded charm and style, on a high and airy hill above Houghton-le-Spring: you find it suddenly, emerging from the murky streets of Philadelphia and Shiney Row. There is an early Methodist *chapel* (1786), with simple stone-gabled front of round-headed windows and an oeil-de-boeuf in the gable; next to it an unexpectedly grand three-storeyed 18th-century brick house with parapet and quoins and long sash windows—now housing the Newbottle Workmen's Social Club Ltd; another good stone house nearby, and Storey House, opposite, simpler but equally dignified. Newbottle is a surprising 18th-century relic, in an ocean of 19th-century industrialism. At the top of the village, at the end of the long narrow green, is an imposing apsidal Victorian *church* (1865).

Newton, Long [17] An agreeable village of one long street—bypassed by the dual carriageway of A66 Stockton to Darlington road. The *church* is of 1856 by S. S. Teulon, and its appearance to the street is unremarkable: a tall narrow nave, with west bellcote. But on the north side of the chancel is the singularly unexpected vaulted mausoleum of the Londonderry family, which makes a memorable addition to the building. Here are buried Vanes, Vane-Tempests and Vane-Tempest-Stewarts (as the family progressed in surnames, wealth and titles). Sir George Vane (knighted 1640), younger brother of Sir Harry Vane of Raby, acquired Long Newton: his grandson, the Revd Sir Henry, who was created a baronet in 1785, married the daughter and heiress of John

Tempest of Wynyard, M.P. for Durham. Their son became Sir Henry Vane-Tempest, father of the redoubtable Frances Anne, who married Charles Stewart, 3rd Marquis of Londonderry, Castlereagh's younger half-brother. There is a monument to Sir Henry Vane-Tempest (d. 1813) by Westmacott; most notable, however (among many family monuments), is that to Lord Londonderry—whose recumbent effigy, originally erected here, was afterwards moved to the private chapel at Wynyard (q.v.). After describing his military prowess as Adjutant General to the Duke of Wellington, and his diplomatic distinction as Ambassador in Vienna, the inscription goes on to tell how 'he exercised a considerable influence in those eventful years which followed the Peace. Called on by his marriage to preside over the vast mining possessions in the County of Durham, he applied to this new field, for the exercise of his energy, the same determined courage and dauntless perseverance which had distinguished his military life. He became the Founder of Seaham Harbour, the Builder of Seaham Town, the Constructor of Seaham & Sunderland Railway; the harbour excavated out of the cliff, on a bare and exposed shore, the town built where not a house had stood, the railways a noble example of the result of unaided private resources. Nor did he in these vast undertakings forget his duties to those he employed; he founded schools, built churches, established the Mechanics' Institute, and provided for the sick by the Seaham Infirmary. A true friend of Civil and Religious Liberty, and an unswerving supporter of Conservative opinions.' Behind the church is the extraordinarily attractive *rectory*, gabled, colour-washed, of 17th- to 18th-century date; and further west along the village street the walled enclosure where once stood Long Newton

The **Penshaw** Monument

church (1876) with bellcote. Old colliery country with odd little hamlets with odd names: Grange Villa is a handful of cottages close to the Twizell Burn to the south; Perkinsville, to the north, suddenly erupted in the 19th century, and is named after the Perkins family of Birtley (q.v.), local colliery owners. And there is an extinct railway line.

Penshaw [4] An odd little village, on high ground—with sprawling, straggling urban outcrops: wide views across the well-wooded oasis of Lambton Park, a public house or two, and a small, blackened, neo-Norman *church* (1830), containing a stone from the Great Pyramid presented by Sir George Elliot, M.P. (*see* West Rainton). One of the most incredible features of County Durham is the Penshaw Monument, which stands on its little hill above the village, conspicuous for miles around, a northern version of the Parthenon. Built of blackened stone, it is a complete Grecian temple—with seven hefty Doric columns to north and south, four to east and west, correct with pediments and frieze and cornice. It was erected in 1842, to the memory of John George Lambton, 1st Earl of Durham (*see* Lambton), by public subscription, and designed by John and Benjamin Green of Newcastle. Its presence here seems at first unfathomable. Instead of the rock of the Acropolis, it stands on a scrubby, grassy hill, with a handful of colliery villages at its feet—Fatfield, Philadelphia, Shiney Row—their very names incredible too; a new bypass on one side, an old railway viaduct on the other. It suddenly appears on the horizon far away, linking County Durham with the Dominion of Canada, a colliery village with the Palace of Westminster. On one occasion Lord Durham's children were driving through Chester-le-Street: 'Lord Durham! Lord Durham for ever!' shouted the crowds. *Life and Letters of the First*

Hall, the home of the Vanes—deserted and demolished when their heirs and successors came in for the greater glories of Wynyard.

Newton Aycliffe [10, 16] The first of the New Towns in County Durham, and begun in 1948. Wide roads, with houses in groups and pairs set among gardens with trees and high hedges give the residential area the pleasant air of a very large country village; grass lines many of the roads, and there are greens and open spaces: the Grenfell Baines group provided the master plan. At the centre of the town is the *church of St Clare*—long and low, with nave and choir and narrow aisles and sanctuary under one roof, and with excellent oak furnishings throughout. The industrial area is equally

well laid out, with factories in spacious surroundings. Newton Aycliffe is in the tradition of Welwyn Garden City—its character friendly, domestic and unassertive.

Pelton [4] The A693 climbs steadily west from Chester-le-Street, and reaches Pelton. A saucy little *church* of 1842 (by John Green) stands in a large churchyard by the side of the road, with tall spiky pinnacles at its four corners, and a diminutive octagonal tower at its west end crowned with a tiny many-gabled spire—a delicious Gothic confection, quite unlike anything built in the middle ages. Rows of terrace cottages: a house opposite the church is named Sabriaco Lodge. West Pelton lies off the main road, with more rows of terrace cottages and a more conventional Victorian

The Transporter Bridge, **Port Clarence**

Earl of Durham by Stuart J. Reid, Longmans, Green & Co., 1906). Here is their tribute to him.

Peterlee [11] The second of the New Towns in County Durham, and named after Peter Lee, miner, County Councillor, Chairman of Durham County Council, President of the Miners' federation and Methodist preacher. Founded in 1947, building began in 1948, with B. Lubetkin as planning consultant. Victor Pasmore, the painter, later became artistic adviser to the Development Corporation—and his hand is to be seen in many of the schemes, in the use of colour or the choice of texture. The town is lucky in its site, a wide natural shallow amphitheatre, with roads running down informally to the centre, where there is a pedestrianized

central square, with large shops and high office blocks. In the residential areas the houses are set in wide lawns; there is none of the seclusion and privacy to be found at Newton Aycliffe. The effect here is quite different, with buildings set in spreading landscapes, with newly planted trees and open spaces. And the scale is different—with houses in groups, and, further away, offices and factories. There is a prominent cruciform *R.C. church*, Our Lady of the Rosary (1966), with green roof, and flèche crowning a low central tower. The *parish church* (St Cuthbert's) is built in a paved garden setting nearer to the centre of the town, with a foundation stone from Lindisfarne laid by Archbishop Ramsey in 1956. Nearby is the Peter Lee Memorial *Methodist church*. To the south-west

is *Shotton Hall*, a late 18th-century stuccoed house, with shallow bow windows and iron balconies, until recently used as the offices of the Peterlee Development Corporation. And a little further south is Castle Eden Dene, the romantic landscape garden created by Rowland Burdon at the very end of the 18th century. Long neglected and overgrown, this now belongs to the corporation, and is being restored, and is open to the public—the greatest possible single asset to the town.

Piercebridge [16] The Roman road from Scotch Corner crosses the Tees here: the George, an admirable hostelry, stands on the Yorkshire side of the river—and a stately three-arched bridge, built in 1789, is the frontier post into

145

County Durham. It is worth descending the river bank behind the George to enjoy the prospect of the Tees, tumbling, bubbling along its wide and rocky bed—with the Durham bank beyond. Across the river the village is grouped round a long rectangular green, on the site of an important Roman station of the 3rd century which covered some eleven acres. Excavation is now in progress behind the cottages on the east side of the green, and fragments discovered here are to be seen in the Bowes Museum, Barnard Castle. The small stone *church* with west bellcote (by Cory and Ferguson) was built in 1873. Just above the road to Gainford (A67) stands *White Cross*, a handsome 18th-century farmhouse with balancing farm buildings to left and right—whitewashed and sparkling like all the farms on the Raby estate.

Pittington [10] It is no use going to the rather gaunt village of this name, on the road from Durham to Hetton-le-Hole, if you are looking for Pittington church—still less exploring New Pittington. Keeping right, drive through both, towards the south-west. The *church* stands at a dead end, in the hamlet of Hallgarth, in trees close to open country. It is worth the search. In origin a Saxon building, the great glory of Pittington is the unique north arcade: four bays of elaborate late Norman work (usually associated with Bishop Pudsey—cf. the Galilee Chapel at Durham), the pillars are alternately octagonal and round, the octagonal being reeded, the round embraced by a snake-like spiral—above, round arches with zigzag ornament. The effect is rich and spectacular. The south arcade is Early English, and above the arcades the small windows are Saxon, and betray the Saxon core. Norman tower, with Early English upper stage; chancel and much 'improvement' (e.g. the two east arches of the north arcade) 1846. Fragments of 12th-century wall painting (Saxon window, north side); tomb of Frosterley marble (south aisle) to one 'nomen (h)abens Christi'—apparently Bishop Pudsey's master mason, named Christian, who is known to have held land here, and is mentioned in the Boldon Book; 13th-century tomb of cross-legged light (north aisle); and (under tower) little 13th-century twin tombs of children. Deep in its plantations to the east, and hard to find in the valley of the Coldburn Beck, off the road from New Pittington to the colliery village of Easington Lane, is *Elemore Hall* (pronounced 'Elly-more'), till 1947 the home of the Baker and later the Baker-Baker family. Built by George Baker between 1749 and 1753, this is an important Palladian house of red brick with stone dressings. The main front of three storeys is crowned with a wide pediment enclosing an elaborate cartouche: the two long extending wings, also of three storeys, are similarly crowned with pediments. A grand flight of steps leads up to the pedimented front door; on the ground floor of the wings are Venetian windows. The family preserved their records carefully: the building accounts name the architect as Robert Shout of Sunderland—and Guiseppe Cortese the plasterer, who executed the elegant plaster ceilings in several downstairs rooms. The house is now a county council special school.

left and opposite **Pittington** church

Raby Castle

◁ The Lower Hall, the Octagon Drawing Room and Larder detail

Pity Me [10] 'Shildon, Spennymoor, Shiney Row, Pelaw, Pity Me, Seldom Seen . . .'—the names of Durham villages are strange, amusing, proverbial, and Pity Me is the best of them all. The explanation of its name is more prosaic: it is a corruption of *petit mere*—a lake or pond that once existed here. There is nothing to see at Pity Me: just a row of dumb cottages, now bypassed by the old North Road (A167), with a back alley or two, a shop or two, and The Tops Hair Salon—which suddenly begins, and with characteristic Durham abruptness suddenly ends. But, of course, it should not be missed.

Port Clarence [17] A fascinating spot – the north landing stage for the *Transporter Bridge*, which crosses the Tees here within a short distance of its mouth. The bridge,

built in 1911, stands 225 feet high, like a great erection made of meccano, and cars are carried across on a ferry, a kind of basket suspended by steel hawsers from the gantry above, the driver being perched in a little cabin aloft. The journey from Middlesbrough to Port Clarence is one not to be missed. In Port Clarence itself are the Clarence Works of the B.S.C Chemical Division, the I.C.I. North Tees Works, the Station Hotel, the Port Clarence General Stores, a little R.C. church—and, towards Haverton Hill, little roads called Eton Terrace, Oxford Terrace, Harrow Terrace and Rugby Terrace. Somehow it seems a far cry from those foundations. For atmosphere Port Clarence should certainly be savoured. The road north from Port Clarence (A178) passes through the strangest, weirdest,

landscape. 'THIS IS A HARD HAT SITE—SAFETY HELMETS MUST BE WORN' declares a notice at the entrance to an industrial site. Nearby are the headquarters of the Teeside Operations of North Sea Petroleum, and on all sides there are chemical works, with steel chimneys like tall masts supported by wires, and pipes sprawling across the ground; nearby again are titanium works, covered with a pall of white powder; across the marsh is the sinister presence of an atomic power station. In the background are the docks at the mouth of the Tees—and, behind, the Cleveland Hills. There are unexpected fields, with cows and horses grazing—and bird-watchers with field glasses following the movements of migratory birds. It is the oddest world.

149

Preston-on-Tees [17] (near Eaglescliffe Junction) The long straight road from Egglescliffe to Stockton (A19)—now much built-up—passes the gates to *Preston Hall*, a plain brick house of 1825, much added to and aggrandized by the Ropner family, the Stockton shipowners, later in the century; there is a handsome Victorian conservatory. It is now a local museum, and old shops have been recreated in the service and stable courts, and cobbled alleyways contrived, redolent of a 19th-century northern town.

Quebec [10] A scattered village along a back road on the exposed hillside south of Lanchester: the odd names of old colliery villages in the county often cause comment—some mark historic events in English history, and Quebec must seem a strange celebration of British arms in distant Canada. Here the collieries are long since closed: a string of cottages and a humble little aisleless Victorian *church* survive. The latter is of stone with a brick chancel, bellcote and roofline of ventilators; interior resplendent with linoleum and riddel posts.

Raby Castle [15] The road north from Staindrop passes the long wall of Raby Park, and soon the castle comes in sight—mediaeval, magnificent and romantic, with its mass of towers, turrets and embattled walls: a great fortified stronghold, which has been continuously inhabited, enlarged, altered and embellished over the centuries from the time of Edward the Confessor to the present day. According to legend, King Cnut (1017–36) built the first castle here (of which perhaps an early bastion remains); through his niece Raby descended to Robert FitzMaldred who married Isabella Neville. It was their son Geoffrey who assumed his mother's name of Neville and was the first Neville of Raby. His son

Ralph was created Lord Neville of Raby and K.G., was the hero of the Battle of Neville's Cross, and died in 1387. His son Ralph was created Earl of Westmorland in 1397, and was father of Cicely, the 'Rose of Raby', who married Richard Plantagenet, Duke of York, and became mother of Edward IV and Richard III, grandmother of Edward V and of Elizabeth, the wife of Henry VII—and so direct ancestress of our present Royal Family. The Nevilles became the most powerful family in County Durham, but the 6th Earl forfeited Raby and all their possessions to the Crown after the disastrous Rising of the Northern Earls in 1569. After a period when Raby was in the possession of the Crown (a Keeper being appointed), the castle was bought in 1626 by Sir Henry Vane, Treasurer of the Household and Principal Secretary of State to Charles I. His son, Sir Henry Vane the Younger, was Treasurer of the Navy and friend of Cromwell; a republican at heart, he nevertheless opposed the execution of the King, and retired to Raby in 1649. But this did not save him at the Restoration: he was taken to the Tower and executed as a traitor. But 'he died', in Pepys' words, 'as much a martyr and saint as ever man did.' His son Christopher was created 1st Lord Barnard of Barnard Castle in 1698. Since then the great Raby estate has been maintained and the castle embellished and glorified in accordance with 18th- and 19th-century taste. The 3rd Lord Barnard was created Earl of Darlington in 1754; the 3rd Earl of Darlington created Duke of Cleveland in 1833. On the extinction of the senior line the Dukedom expired in 1891, and the younger line (descended from a brother of the 1st Earl of Darlington) succeeded to the barony of Barnard. The 9th Lord Barnard married a daughter of the 3rd Marquis of Exeter, who was herself descended from the 1st Earl of Westmor-

land—so in this century the owners of Raby have once more Neville blood flowing in their veins. The present owner is the 11th Lord Barnard, who became Lord Lieutenant of County Durham in 1970. The approach to the castle across the park is particularly beautiful: the towers and turrets appear and disappear among the trees—and now the *gatehouse* (14th century) is upon us, with its little stone figures standing on the battlements. Through the gatehouse stands the awesome and dominating *Clifford's Tower*, and it is worth walking round the outside of the castle to survey the towers and gateways. The bulk of the building is 14th century (the licence to crenellate was granted in 1378), though fragments—as has been said—date back to the 12th century or earlier. If we turn left at Clifford's Tower, which stands in front of the Inner Keep, we pass the *Kitchen Tower*, and *Mount Raskelf*, and come to the *Chapel Tower*, the centrepiece of the east front. In the 18th century this was transformed into a gatehouse to allow carriages to pass through from the inner courtyard: there had been originally only a postern gate here. Beyond the Chapel Tower is *Bulmer's Tower*, the oldest part of the castle: originally free-standing, the base is 12th century, and traditionally incorporates King Cnut's bastion, but certainly takes its name from Bertram de Bulmer, grandfather of Isabella Neville. Round the corner of Bulmer's Tower we find the 19th-century south front of the castle: this is dominated by the *Octagon Tower*, built in the 1840s by William Burn; the great windows above light the Barons' Hall, those below the Drawing Room. This front contains the domestic quarters, formed in the 18th and 19th centuries; and at the west end is *Joan's Tower*, named after Joan Beaufort, wife of the 1st Earl of Westmorland. The west front is dominated by the

Redmarshall church, 17th-century furniture and fossilized shells on the font

Neville Gateway. This is the principal entrance to the Inner Court and so to the house itself. In the 1760s a great entrance was formed into the Lower Hall by John Carr of York to allow carriages to drive through the hall, and out again under the Chapel Tower. The Inner Court is cool and cobbled: the keep, the long line of the windows of the Baron's Hall, the surrounding towers, the castle clock—these provide the setting of what Leland called 'ye hart of ye castell'. There is one more tower beyond the Neville Gateway—the *Watch Tower*—and we are back at Clifford's Tower once more. The entrance for visitors is the garden door at the foot of Joan's Tower. From here a delightful tour of the principal rooms may be made. The *Small Drawing Room* and the *Library* are 18th-century rooms: handsome chimneypieces, panelling, plasterwork, splendid furniture, pictures and china—all of a domestic scale—lead on to the grander rooms created by Burn in the 19th century. The *Ante-Library*, the *Octagon Drawing Room* and the *Dining Room* are all his work and redolent of the period: magnificent French furniture, sumptuous china, chandeliers, silk-covered walls, a great set of family portraits—these are the state rooms *par excellence*. And from the Dining Room we descend to the *Lower Hall*. This long, pillared, vaulted, Gothic Hall was originally built in the 14th century, but is now virtually the work of Carr, working in his less familiar Gothick mode. He heightened the room and vaulted it in plaster, all in the style of the 14th century. But the style is restrained, the atmosphere solemn. And above is the *Barons' Hall*; the tremendous room where

Seven hundred knights, retainers all / Of Neville, at their master's call / Had sate together in Raby's Hall

(in Wordsworth's words) is really the re-creation of William Burn,

151

who lengthened it by 52 feet, formed the great windows at the south end, and added the heavily timbered roof. The stone minstrels' gallery at the north end is, however, mediaeval and unusual. There is heraldic glass by Willement, and a great gathering of portraits. The whole scale of the room is magnifical. A door at the north end leads into the chapel: restored by Burn, and redecorated in 1901, its atmosphere is Victorian, though in fact the vaulting, and the arcading of the west wall, are mediaeval. Perhaps the finest room in the castle is the *Kitchen*. With its 14th-century vaulted roof and louvre, its windows pierced through the thickness of the walls, its stone-flagged floors, its great fireplaces, its bleached furniture and sets of kitchen utensils, the room is light and airy, reminiscent of that other great mediaeval kitchen at Stanton Harcourt. A further succession of stone passages leads to the *Steward's Room* and the *Servants' Hall*—long, low and vaulted, set with its long table and benches. Here, perhaps, may be savoured the throbbing life of Raby through the centuries. On the west side of the castle, in Neville's Gateway, in the Watch Tower and in Clifford's Tower, James Paine formed notable rooms for the 1st Earl of Darlington in the early 18th century. The Hunter's Gallery, a long curving corridor on the first floor, decorated in a delightful pre-Strawberry Hill Gothick, connects the Watch Tower with the former state rooms in Clifford's Tower, where in irregular shaped apartments Paine formed elegant Palladian rooms replete with handsome woodwork and elaborate Rococo plaster decoration by Perritt of York. But in the 19th century the new state rooms on the south side supplanted these—which were relegated to bedrooms—and this part of the castle is not shown to visitors. Across a wide stretch of grass to the north are the gardens and stables.

The *stables* are a particular delight: built by John Carr, they comprise a chaste Palladian façade with arcaded front and low pavilion towers, and contain a remarkable collection of coaches and carriages. Walled gardens, bounded by a ha-ha, provide the perfect setting from which to survey the park with its lake and herds of deer—the castle, austere and solemn, presiding over all.

Rainton, East [10] Old colliery country: it was here—and across to Hetton—that the great East Durham coal mines were established in the early 19th century. The village lies to the south of the main Sunderland to Durham dual carriageway (A690). Inconspicuous *church* of 1866.

Rainton, West [10] The tall Victorian spire is a prominent landmark on the road (A690) from Durham to Sunderland: it is an odd experience to enter the *church* and read the inscription recording that the tower and spire were the gift of Sir George Elliot, M.P. (1877), and that the tablet recording the fact is a block of granite from the Great Pyramid of Ghizeh. The church (by E. R. Robson 1864) is grand and lofty: two arches from the Dominican Priory at Newcastle were re-erected outside the north transept. The great East Durham coal mines were developed in this neighbourhood in the early 19th century: Lord Londonderry's Rainton colliery covered an area of some 4,000 acres, and it was to transport his coal from these collieries that he built the harbour at Seaham. Sir George Elliot was for many years chief viewer of Lord Londonderry's Rainton collieries, and in charge of his enterprises at Seaham. Starting life, at the age of 10, as trapper boy at Whitefield Colliery, Penshaw, he raised himself by means of night school, where he studied surveying and mine engineering; and later developed his own mining interests

in Wales. Later still he manufactured the first telegraph cables which spanned the Atlantic. He became M.P. for North Durham in 1868, financial adviser to the Khedive of Egypt, and a great favourite of Disraeli. He was made a baronet in 1874 (*see also* Penshaw).

Redmarshall [17] A small village, only a few miles north-west of Stockton, with a tall gabled Victorian rectory adjoining the east end of the church, an outcrop of new bijou residences, and the Ship Inn. The *church* has a Norman tower with Perpendicular battlemented top, Norman chancel arch, Norman south door, and a wide south chapel like a single transept, added in the 13th century, and containing the effigy of Thomas de Langton (d. 1440) of Wynyard, and his wife. 15th-century sedilia and Easter sepulchre in chancel; 17th-century pews and altar rails.

Rokeby [15] (pronounced Rookby) A long stone wall bordering the A66, a beautifully planted park, a pair of Palladian gate piers at the corner of the by-road—with a glimpse of an apricot-coloured house through the iron screen—that, to the passing motorist, is Rokeby. Rokeby was built for himself by Sir Thomas Robinson, amateur architect and dilettante, Member of Parliament and Governor of Barbados, and was completed in 1731. William Robinson, merchant of London, had begun acquiring property here in the early 17th century, from the Rokeby family. Sir Thomas—'Long Sir Tom'—was born in 1700, inherited in 1720, and soon set about planning a new house. The house he built is an exceedingly beautiful one, in the purest Palladian taste: a compact central block with pedimented centrepiece, a lower wing to each side set far back, a still lower wing

Rokeby

beyond that set still further back. All are pyramid-roofed, and the centre of each block is accentuated by a single dignified feature: a low pediment with a round-headed window set in a blind arcade at the extremities, a pedimented window on the first floor in the middle blocks, and a low Doric portico with pedimented window above it in the house itself. At the back two squat towers (à la Kent at Holkham), again with pyramid roofs, frame the centre of the main block: it is a remarkable composition of diminishing cubes and low-pitched pyramids, at once subtle and serene. The windows are widely spaced, and the principal rooms are on the *piano nobile*. The main front is faced in ashlar, but the side façades are stuccoed and painted with a gorgeous apricot wash. On a warm sunny day—indeed on any day—it is difficult not to imagine oneself looking at one of Palladio's own villas, on the banks of the Brenta. Robinson's extravagances led to his selling Rokeby in 1769 to John Sawrey Morritt, whose descendants still live here. The purchaser's son, J. B. S. Morritt, M.P., was the close

friend of Scott and Southey, and himself a collector of note: it was he who acquired the celebrated *Rokeby Venus* (by Velasquez), now in the National Gallery. The front door, under the Doric portico, leads into a low pillared hall, à la Palladio, with the *Library* on its right. Behind the hall is a long vestibule with apsidal ends, reminiscent of the Gallery at Chiswick House, with an oval garden hall at the west end, the staircase at the east. Upstairs, pride of place goes to the *Saloon*. This splendid room, rising to the full height of the house, has a richly decorated groined ceiling, grand 18th-century chimneypiece, and great pedimented doorway in the north wall ('My chief expense has been in Palladian doors and windows', wrote Long Sir Tom to his father-in-law, the Earl of Carlisle, in 1731); 'Fay ce que vouldras' proclaims the motto from Rabelais inscribed on the entablature of this one. Fine period features adorn all the rooms of the *piano nobile*; the *Music Room* leads out of the Saloon, and the *Dining Room* occupies the first floor of the west wing. This room, redecorated in Adam style at the end of the 18th century, has a

wide apsidal recess for the fireplace, and delicate neo-classical decoration. Perhaps the most charming room of all is the *Breakfast Room* on the ground floor opposite the Library. Here the walls are decorated with prints (in the manner of the print rooms at Woodhall Park and Uppark): the long low proportions of the room, the many windows facing south and west, the gracious Palladian features, all combine to provide the perfect apartment. Indeed the whole house, mellow and beautiful, casts a rare spell. The great surprise of Rokeby, on a sunny day in spring, is to catch a glimpse through the trees on the eastern edge of the park of what appears to be a small mediaeval castle: a folly tower, built perhaps by Long Sir Tom? But no, it is *Mortham Tower*, the genuine 14th-century tower-house of the Rokeby family. The tower itself stands in the north-west corner of a little courtyard, which is enclosed on the south by an embattled wall and low arched gateway, heavily buttressed. Later wings were added in Tudor times round the other sides of the courtyard—perhaps a Great Hall which

Seaham Harbour

has disappeared. But what survives contains remarkable, romantic rooms with many original features: it stands close to the spot where the Greta flows into the Tees in a setting remarkable and romantic in itself. On the A66, in a lonely spot west of Rokeby Park, stands the *church*, a small, pedimented, stone Palladian building with a bellcote, consecrated in 1778. It is so similar to that little church of flint at Glynde in Sussex which Sir Thomas Robinson built for Bishop Trevor in 1763 (*see* Bishop Auckland) that this must be by him also. A chancel was added in 1877, so the interior is very different from that at Glynde. It contains one Robin-

son monument (1777) by Nollekens, another to J. S. Morritt (1815) by Westmacott, and two others, one to J. B. S. Morritt (1823), Scott's friend. The Victorian east window is by Gibbs. (*See also* Greta Bridge.)

Romaldkirk [14/15] A village of diverse lanes and diverse greens, with groups of stone cottages or larger houses set in a friendly haphazard fashion round the greens, and lanes leading off to Middleton-in-Teesdale, or to Eggleston, or to Cotherstone, or up to the wild moors. Trees and gardens and stone walls set off all to perfection. The *church* and Geor-

gian *rectory* preside over the lowest green. Distinguished church, with long, highly ornamental Decorated chancel, embattled and pinnacled, wide south transept and embattled Perpendicular tower. The interior is, alas, scraped—the stonework all 'snail-pointed'—but it is fine and spacious. Impressive late 12th-century arcades with round arches and tall round piers; good Decorated tracery, but an odd unsophisticated Perpendicular east window. Early 18th-century pulpit with sounding board and elegant staircase—but the other parts of the 'three-decker' unfortunately dismantled and banished to the north aisle. Monuments to the recusant

154

Maire family of Lartington in north transept—one married a Bedingfeld of Oxburgh—and notable tomb nearby to Sir Hugh Fitz-Henry, Lord of Cotherstone (d. 1305); 12th-century font with Jacobean cover; gloomy Victorian glass in south transept (to the Agent of the Strathmores at Streatlam, 1867). A rewarding building.

Rookhope [8] A narrow lane from Eastgate leads up a solitary moorland valley to this small industrial village. Terraces of workers' cottages are dominated by the aluminium works, and a little Victorian church stands on higher ground behind. It is a lonely, isolated little community. And further on, outside the village to the north, a still more unexpected sight—robust stone arches, like Roman arcades in a deserted, overgrown forum—stand inexplicably in the narrow valley. In reality they are 19th-century relics of the old lead-mining industry.

Ryhope [5] Sunderland extends relentlessly along the coast: the Victorian colliery village grew up inland. But there are some vestiges of the older village round the green—and there is an imposing Victorian *church* (1870 by T. C. Ebdy) with prominent tower. But the most notable thing at Ryhope is the Victorian *Pumping Station*, which stands like a great Flemish Gothic town hall, with a lower attendant gabled wing and tall chimney in its own well-tended grounds. Within are two huge beam engines. It has been splendidly restored to working order as an industrial monument, and is open to the public.

Ryton [3] Interminable traffic along the A695: the sequestered village with its green, standing high above the south bank of the River Tyne, is a delightful surprise. Victorian houses line the main road: in the village itself are many older houses and cottages. *Ryton Grove* is a

handsome house of 1742, of brick with stone dressings and sash windows; there is also a charming, smaller, white house with Venetian windows. And south of the church is the imposing and enormous former *Rectory*. The Georgianized east front with sash windows conceals an Elizabethan core: mullioned windows and early masonry are apparent on the garden side. The *church* is one of the best in the county, and is dominated by its great 13th-century lead spire. Comparable with Long Sutton in colour and texture, and reminiscent of the (shingle-covered) broach spire of Horsham in shape and silhouette, it crowns a massive west tower: wide 'engaged' aisles, wide nave, long chancel with lancet windows and east end with three lancets and one 'vesica' above— the east end is a careful restoration. The low nave and much Victorian glass result in a dark interior. 17th-century 'Cosin' chancel screen; 16th-century continental carved figures on altar rails; late 13th-century effigy of a deacon wearing dalmatic, in sanctuary; two small late 16th-century brasses to Bunny family (two generations held the living), and later monuments to rectors in chancel. Beautiful churchyard: on the south side is a view of the west front of the former rectory with its large garden; on the north side the steep well-wooded banks lead down to the Tyne. Along the main road to the east is the handsome little late 19th-century *church of St Hilda* (by Oliver and Leeson, 1889) with its squat tower. And two miles to the west along the main road the suburban growth at last comes to an end. Open country begins, and across a lovely park, close to the Northumberland frontier, stands *Bradley Hall*. Built c. 1750 for the Simpson family, and ascribed (without documentary evidence) to James Paine, the south front is seven bays wide, with broad pediment across the three central bays-

—Paine's favourite pediment motif—and large, less-regular work behind. Bradley is still a private residence, and the home of the Simpson family—a remarkable oasis.

Sacriston [10] Smell of coal: Sacriston Grange Colliery is busy at the north end of the village. In mediaeval times Sacriston manor was attached to the Sacrist of the Cathedral: hence the name. Fragments of the mediaeval manor house remain in an old farmhouse at Sacriston Heugh, behind the woods beyond the colliery. The two long streets of the 19th-century village meet at the crossroads, and comprise the usual amalgam of odd buildings: Victorian terraces, rows of council houses, the Sacriston Memorial Institute (with wooden shack-like clock turret), a cinema (closed), a cemetery (with SACRISTON CEMETERY in large lettering in the iron entrance arch), a Methodist chapel, a little Roman Catholic church, the parish church, and some farm buildings in the middle of it all, with 'Accredited Herd' on the door of the cow house. The *parish church* is of 1863, with a bell on a wooden bracket at the west end; well-detailed, spacious interior with apse, with larger window at east end.

Sadberge [16] On rising ground, bypassed by the dual carriageway of the A66 Darlington to Stockton road, and with wide views. A pretty tree-lined village green, on which stands a great stone boulder. 'This stone was placed here' reads the inscription, 'to commemorate the Golden Jubilee of Victoria, Queen of the United Kingdom, Empress of India, and Countess of Sadberge, 1867.' Few such obscure villages can claim such distinction. Sadberge was in the middle ages a royal manor of importance: the earldom is indeed attached to the Crown. The small stone *church* of 1831 contains a few fragments of its mediaeval predecessor built into the south porch, rescued—oddly—from a public house in Darlington. Sadberge specializes in the unlikely.

St John's Chapel [8] or St John Weardale, to give it its ancient name, is a small town with a diminutive classical Town Hall surveying the wide grassy square—the church on one side, stone houses and small shops, an inn or two (notably the Golden Lion) on the other: the road from Stanhope proceeds to still wilder country to the west. The *church* was built in 1752; low west tower with pyramid roof, the interior with great Tuscan columns supporting a shallow domed ceiling, and some colourful enamelled glass. *Ireshopeburn* is a hamlet to the west, where there is a tall early 17th-century house with mullioned windows, called *Newhouse*, built against the hillside. Memorial to John Wesley at the corner of the main road.

Satley [9] Countrified and unsophisticated little village on the uplands between Lanchester and Wolsingham, with small Victorian *church* with plain west tower. Simple, well-furnished interior entered under deep west gallery. Mediaeval fragments built into the west wall.

Seaham [5] The terraces of miners' cottages and later council houses rise and fall along the contours of the low undulating hills which lead down to the sea: the approach to Seaham is pretty drab. But the broad green sward overlooking the sea and the little harbour is undoubtedly attractive. The story of the founding of Seaham Harbour by Charles Vane-Tempest-Stewart, 3rd Marquis of Londonderry, is told in detail in *Aristocrat in Business* (edited by R. W. Sturgess, Durham County Local History Society, 1975). Lord Stewart (as he then was) purchased the Seaham Estate from Sir Ralph

Milbanke (8th Bt) in 1821. Milbanke, father-in-law of Byron, had extensive coal interests, and had already envisaged founding a harbour here to be called Port Milbanke: these ideas Londonderry took over, and developed. With the help of John Biddle, his agent, he employed the engineer William Chapman (who had already drawn out a scheme for Milbanke) to produce plans for a harbour at Dalden Ness in 1823; these were later revised by Rennie and Telford, the leading engineers of their day. Meantime estimates for the work soared, and Londonderry was faced with raising immense capital—but finally work started in 1828 on 'a work which no individual, *save one*, would have the courage to undertake in these eventful times' (so Biddle wrote). Work went on in 1829 and 1830: quays were built, piles were sunk for the piers and harbour walls, railway lines constructed to connect the new harbour with the collieries inland, and the first coals were loaded on a new collier, named *Lord Seaham*, which proudly sailed out of the new port in 1831. Work proceeded for four more years: by 1835 the Outer Harbour, North Harbour, Light Vessel Harbour and Wet Dock were complete. Yet the imposing new town which Londonderry had dreamed of was never built. In 1828 John Dobson had drawn out plans for a grand hotel, for offices and shops and a fine sea front; these, alas, were never built—and a modest little town, with modest little houses, grew up instead. The town is indeed drab: pedestrian shopping streets surround the harbour *church* (by John Prosser, 1835) with its pinnacled tower and commissioners' style plan. Along the front are dowdy little shops and the Harbour View Hotel. At the north end some attractive-looking stuccoed houses—which might have strayed from Worthing—face the long wide green, in the centre of which stand

the former Londonderry Offices (now the *police station*), a stone Classical building with sash windows and a central clock tower crowned with a low dome. 'PLAYING OF GAMES PROHIBITED' proclaims a notice nearby. The only other building to note is the *Londonderry Institute* in Tempest Place, a single-storey building with wide-pedimented Doric portico, now somewhat down-at-heel. Towards the end of his life the Marquis sank a large mine—the Vane-Tempest—to the north of the town, close to the coast. Beyond this stands the *old church* of Seaham village, an important little building crouching on the low cliff, looking out to sea, with a long low nave, long low chancel and low embattled tower. The nave is earliest Norman or latest Saxon: the chancel and tower Early English. The chancel has a piscina comprising two small arches—at the back of one of which is carved a hand raised in blessing. And close to the church stands *Seaham Hall*, now a hospital. Victorianized and stuccoed, it is in fact the late-Georgian house built by Sir Ralph Milbanke as a seaside residence, an appendage to Halnaby (*see* Hurworth). Except for a single fine chimneypiece there are few relics of those days. Yet it was here, in 1815, in the Drawing Room, that Lord Byron married Anna Isabella Milbanke. 'It is impossible' wrote Sir Timothy Eden, 'to fit in the shiny linoleum floor, the aspidistra, and the waiting room furniture with any memory of the moody poet' (*Durham*, Robert Hale, 1951). From here bride and bridegroom drove to Halnaby for the first night of their much regretted marriage. Seaham is indeed a trifle melancholy.

Seaton Carew [12] A strange and unexpected little seaside resort between Hartlepool and the mouth of the Tees: its heyday was the early 19th century, when rows of pretty little stucco houses were built along the front and round the green, a modest square open to the sea. Some have Gothick features, some are plain Regency, but all are modest. It is of the scale of Littlehampton: it never aspired to the grandeur of Brighton or Scarborough, or the elegance of Sidmouth—and since its early flowering it has decayed quietly, but still presents a face of faded charm. The 20th century has added little but a few ice cream parlours and some cheap seaside amusements. There is a Commissioners' type *church* of 1831 (by Thomas Pickersgill), with west tower and broad aisleless nave, in a back street, with wide views across the flat countryside behind. Along the coast road towards Hartlepool are wide green swards—with menacing chimneys peering over the low-rising ground facing the sea: industry is never far away.

Sedgefield [11] In the green open country between Durham and Stockton, Sedgefield is a small town of Georgian houses and wide greens, presided over by a church with splendid tower. Only in the distance are there signs of industry—the factories and the cooling towers of Billingham and Hartlepool far away to the east, and the jolly little flaming chimney of the Fishburn coking works closer at hand to the north. But Sedgefield is rural England. The town is now bypassed, and the swirling traffic to Tyne or Tees rushes on its way along the new roads outside, leaving the streets intact, streets of brick and pantile, of small houses and cottages mostly, but enlivened by a few larger ones. The *Manor House* (now District Council offices) is tall and handsome with its sash windows and pedimented front door. Wide greens lead up to the *parish church*. A grand Perpendicular tower, an Early English nave with clustered columns and stiff-leaf capitals, a Decorated chancel and transepts with windows of cur-

vilinear tracery—all this is satisfying. But the glory of the building is the 'Cosin' furnishing. Dennis Granville, Cosin's son-in-law and afterwards Dean of Durham, became rector here in 1667, and the exquisite woodwork of the chancel must be due to him. Canopied stalls and panelling, richly carved desks and poppyheads, the screen formed of open canopies and crowned with a tiara of Gothic pinnacles resting on Classical shafts to left and right of the entrance—here is the remarkable combination of Gothic and Classical, so redolent of 17th-century High Anglican piety, and unique to County Durham. The devout intimacy of the chancel is further enhanced by an early 18th-century organ, marble floor and monuments. There are two 15th-century 'shroud' brasses in the north aisle; one notable early 14th-century brass of a kneeling lady in the south transept was stolen, but has been recovered; the octagonal font is 15th century. South of the church stands the former *rectory*, a distinguished house of 1793, built by Bishop Barrington. The entrance front is nicely proportioned, with central doorway and fanlight, slightly extruding bays on either side, and a short recessed wing at each end. On the garden side these wings contain bow windows on the ground floor, and the centre of the house is crowned by a low wide pediment; the gardens slope down to a small lake. A tablet over the front door records

Munificentia
Samuelis et Shute Barrington
quorum unus
Classis Britannicae Praefectus
alter
Ecclesiae Dunelmensis Episcopus.

The Barringtons were a notable and gifted family: of the sons of the first Viscount, one was an admiral, and one Bishop of Durham (see inscription above), another a general, and the eldest son a Cabinet minister and Chancellor

of the Exchequer. The Bishop's nephew (afterwards 5th Viscount) was Prebendary of Durham and Rector of Sedgefield; it was for him that this house was built. South of the town is the racecourse, and, nearby, *Sands Hall*—a tall good-looking house of 1738 with lower wings. To the west of the Durham road is *Hardwick Hall*. Hardwick was notable for the great landscape garden laid out here by John Burdon, who bought the place in 1748. A lake of 36 acres was surrounded by lawns and well-wooded walks. James Paine was commissioned to build a great temple, a banqueting house, a Gothick seat and other delights. He also designed a great Palladian mansion, with long windows on the *piano nobile*, and attendant pedimented wings. The house was never built: John Burdon overspent on his garden, and a modest house of no great distinction, perhaps incorporating an older building, had to do service instead. In 1780 he sold the place to William Russell (*see* Brancepeth)—keeping a life interest in the house for himself. During this century the gardens have decayed, and the garden buildings have been at the mercy of vandals. The Gothick seat has gone; the Banqueting House, purest essay in Palladianism by Paine, has also gone. Only the temple survives—in a shattered state. An open four-square Ionic colonnade surrounded an octagon, which was surmounted by a great dome: within, a great room was decorated with marble and stucco (by Cortese). It commanded a wide view westwards across the county. Now the house is an hotel, and the park has been taken over by the county council, to be opened (and restored) as a country park. It is much to be hoped that this rare and precious temple may yet be saved. The lake is silted up, but the serpentine canal is being dredged and the woodland walks reclaimed. Something may survive of John Burdon's paradise.

Shadforth [11] Unexpectedly rural—now that the collieries are closed—and a village prettily set on either side of a long green. Many of the cottages are now smartened-up for 'commuter' residents. The Victorian *church* is away to the north, on rising ground, opposite council houses—a barn of a church, with wide nave and narrow chancel and bellcote, but well furnished and devotional.

Sherburn [10] Sherburn Hospital was founded by Bishop Pudsey in 1181 for sixty-five lepers, and refounded as an almshouse by Bishop Langley in 1434. The 13th-century *Gatehouse* leads into a wide quadrangle of lawns and trees; on the left is a long low range of 18th-century buildings for the almoners, on the right a dignified house of 1833 for the Master, and opposite a large gabled Victorian hospital block—with the *chapel* alongside. This dates back to the original foundation; the lower part of the square battlemented west tower is Norman, the upper part Early English, with two elegant tiers of lancets and trefoil-arched arcades. The chapel was largely rebuilt in 1868 (by Austin and Johnson) in Norman style, the three west bays of the south wall alone being original. A mile to the north-east is Sherburn village, which grew up in the 19th century to serve the local colliery. Victorian *church* (1872) with quite a grand little octagonal steeple on north side.

Shields, South [5] stands in a magnificent position at the mouth of the Tyne. Here in the early 2nd century A.D., in the reign of the Emperor Hadrian, the Romans built a fort, a marine outpost of Hadrian's Wall, as part of their great defensive system of northern England. It is a pleasure today to stand here at the mouth of the estuary, watch the shipping entering or

Sedgefield

leaving the Tyne, and look across to North Shields and Tynemouth on the opposite bank. In the past two hundred years South Shields has grown tremendously: it has absorbed adjacent villages like Westoe and Harton to the south, and the industrial growth between here and Jarrow to the west is continuous. The oldest buildings in the town today are the Old Town Hall (1768) and the tower of the parish church of the same date; both stand in the market place, and this is the ideal place from which to start our tour of the town. The *Old Town Hall*, with its domed cupola and open arches supported on Tuscan columns is a little building of charm: it is unfortunate that the whole square has been rebuilt in recent years in the dullest style, and now provides a characterless setting for this distinguished little building. But on the south side stands the *parish church of St Hilda*, an 18th-century rebuilding of the mediaeval church, built perhaps in the place where St Hilda established a nunnery in the 7th century. The tower is of 1768, the rest of the church of 1810, in latest Classical, with the interior recently gaily redecorated. There are ample galleries round three sides, with nave and aisles separated by cast-iron arches and pillars. There is a shallow apsidal sanctuary, and a marble font of 1675 by Robert Trollop of Newcastle. From here it is a short walk down to the riverside. There are old warehouses, and a public house called the Neptune Hotel: Mill Dam leads to the cobbled *Corporation Quay*, presided over by an imposing pillared, pedimented Victorian building of blackened stone, standing on an open arcade: this is now unoccupied, and the lion and unicorn in the pediment are crumbling and broken. Next to this stand the offices of the River Police, also in blackened stone, with bay-windowed façade: from the

Sedgefield

South Shields town hall

able tombstones (such as that dedicated by an officer called Barates to his freedwoman wife Regina), an altar or two, and many household or military utensils. In Mile End Road nearby is the *railway station* with its Gothic front and rose window; the Station Hotel opposite has a little overhanging corner turret in Scottish Baronial taste; and now we are at the crossroads at the centre of the town. King Street (west) leads back to the market place: Ocean Road (east) towards the sea. But carrying straight on we soon see the new *town hall*, at the corner of Beach Road, designed by E. E. Fetch in 1903. Ionic columns, a rusticated base, sash windows, a central pediment with reclining figures lying nonchalantly at its sides against the higher balustraded crest—the whole has the full flavour of Edwardian Baroque. At the north-west corner is the tall clock tower, with domed top and great standing figures at the corners, with a further flourish of Ionic columns capped with urns, and a golden galleon weather-vane. This monumental building is the finest display of civic pride in the county. Turning east along Beach Road we pass some pleasant early 19th-century terraces, and reach the sea front. Here are Victorian seaside villas and terraces, the Marine Park, and (notable in the history of South Shields) the *clock tower* to the memory of Henry Greathead and William Wouldhave, the inventors of the lifeboat. Behind, under a canopy, is displayed a lifeboat of 1833. Returning to the centre of the town by way of Ocean Road, we pass the *Marine Technical College* (Tudor, in red brick and stone) and, opposite, the *Public Library and Museum*. Taking the A19 south we come to the old village street of *Westoe*. Here, in a well-treed enclave, are two terraces of 18th- and 19th-century houses—the fashionable residential district at that time. And *St Michael's, South Westoe*, is an interesting and

quayside are wide views up and down the river. The road east that hugs the river climbs the low cliffs: there is a narrow terrace of late Georgian houses called Green's Place—the finest of them, with a porch, is the Pilot Master's Office. And now we are on the wide open space of the Lawe, overlooking the entrance to the Tyne. The pier is below; opposite is Tynemouth with the Priory ruins a prominent landmark, and the great statue of Admiral Collingwood also visible. The Lawe was the site of the Roman fort: now a modest terrace of Victorian seaside villas leads

down along the front; and there is a tall brick obelisk, one of a pair of navigation marks, a public house called the Harbour Lights, and another called the Beacon—to keep up the nautical air. To see anything of the Roman remains it is necessary to make our way inland by one of the narrow streets to what is called *Roman Remains Park*. Here we can see the layout of Arbeia, the foundations of walls and gates, of granaries and barracks—and inspect the small *museum* opened in 1953 by Sir Mortimer Wheeler. This contains a number of important exhibits, including some not-

Tynemouth seen across the mouth of the river from **South Shields**

original work by Austin Johnson and Hicks (1882) in red brick in the late-Perpendicular style, the interior specially ornate with a heavy hammer-beam roof. *Harton*, beyond, has an agreeable stone aisleless church of 1864, with south porch tower with polygonal spire. From here it is possible to drive east along the B1300 to Marsden Bay. Here are wide green swards along the whole coastline south from South Shields. The odd thing is that the long line of houses here do not face the sea as is the way with most seaside housing: they face inland—with their back gardens and washing lines facing the coast. The Marsden Rocks, close to the cliffs, are craggy and awe-inspiring,

the haunt of kittiwakes and other sea birds. In a grotto, burrowed out of the cliffs in the 19th century, is an unexpected restaurant. And at Souter Point, almost at Whitburn, is the attractive *lighthouse* (1871) with its attendant houses.

Shildon [10] is more or less contiguous with St Andrew Auckland and Bishop Auckland (q.v.), and represents some of the oldest industrial country in County Durham. There are a few old cottages in the old village: here stands the *church*, originally built in 1833, but greatly enlarged with a west tower with low pyramid cap, and wide aisles, in 1900; spacious, effective interior. To the south the main street leads

down past the public gardens and bandstand, to St John's Road, which leads to the *Timothy Hackworth Museum*, and that most historic railway line in the world, where the first passenger train was set on its way on 27 September 1825, and the celebrated Stockton and Darlington Railway established. The principal holy places for the pilgrim are *Soho House*, where Timothy Hackworth lived from 1840 to his death in 1850, as proprietor of the Soho Engine Works—this is now the Hackworth Museum, opened by the Queen Mother in 1975, which is exceedingly attractive and full of interesting things; the old *Pattern Shop* of the Soho works (the only building still

Westoe, **South Shields**

standing)—which is just the other side of the railway line; and the *Masons' Arms Crossing*, further along the line. An inscription on a building nearby records 'From Shildon near this site the Stockton and Darlington Railway Company on 27 September 1825 ran the first passenger train drawn by a steam engine.' Hackworth, friend and associate of George Stephenson, built his first steam engine in 1811—a year or two before Stephenson built his—though it

was Stephenson's 'Locomotion Nº 1' that pulled the first train in 1825. His famous *Royal George* was built and came into service in 1827. He is buried in the churchyard up the hill, and there is a statue of him in the public gardens. To the south of the railway line is New Shildon, where there is a vintage Victorian *church* of 1869 at the end of a gloomy little street. It has an apsidal east end, and an extraordinary gargoyle-encrusted broach spire: quite a powerful building.

Shincliffe [10] Bypassed by the A177 (Durham to Stockton)—a pretty village street, though many of its cottages are now spruced-up for 'commuter' residents. Victorian *church* (1870) with solid spire. Good views of Durham Cathedral.

Shiney Row [4] The quintessence of the old mining communities between Chester-le-Street and Houghton-le-Spring: coal has been mined here for centuries, and carried along the River Wear from the

Westoe, South Shields

staiths in keels to Sunderland and
the sea. Despite the euphemistic
name, it is a world of drab terraces,
old public houses, much loved
but dim little churches, railway
lines and (with the extinction of
the old collieries) new industries.
One place merges with the
next—Fatfield, Fence Houses,
Philadelphia—but they are all the
same. On one side is the amazing
oasis of Lambton Park—and the
whole scene is presided over by the
Penshaw Monument; the aristocra-

tic jostles with the plebeian—they
have lived side by side for centuries,
and are interdependent.

Shotley Bridge [3] A beautiful
well-wooded stretch of the River
Derwent, which here divides
County Durham from Northumberland; the bridge is a single span
of 1838. Rows of cottages and
houses climb the steep hill, and the
Crown and Cross Swords at the
corner of the village commemorates
its long connection with sword

making. It was in the late 17th century that sword makers from Sol-
ingen in Germany settled here: the
families of Oley and Mohl made
Shotley Bridge famous, and sword
making continued here until well
into the 19th century. A terrace of
small houses on the road from
Blackhill bears the inscription
(above nos. 22 and 23)

O

W   A

1787

163

for W. and A. Oley. The last member of the Oley family died only twenty years ago. Above the village in a dramatic position stands the *church* by John Dobson of Newcastle (1850), in his Early English style with broach spire; the north aisle is an addition of 1881 by J. Walton Wilson. Well-furnished interior, with two windows by Wailes (south aisle). The revolving 'hotel' door under the tower is an unusual feature for a church. Half-way down the hill the remarkable *Lloyds Bank* building, with its High Victorian gothic details, was originally built as Town Hall and Assembly Rooms.

Shotton [11] New Shotton is the colliery village to the west of Peterlee: there is a blackened mid-Victorian church (1863) without even a bellcote; the figure of a soldier for a war memorial; and a derelict colliery and slag heap. Shotton Hall is now engulfed in Peterlee (q.v.).

Silksworth [5] Now all part of outer-Sunderland, but a fragment of the old village survives—with a handsome Edwardian *Hall* (now a restaurant), and a few old cottages nearby. New Silksworth grew up in the 19th century round the colliery: Victorian *church* (1868).

Sockburn [16] There is a turning off the narrow road that leads from Neasham to Low Dinsdale marked 'SOCKBURN only'; after a time the road peters out into a farm track, and there are notices marked 'Sockburn Hall PRIVATE' or 'No Parking'. On the right is a good-looking Georgian red-brick farmhouse across a field. Wordsworth and his sister stayed here in 1799 with their Hutchinson cousins, and Wordsworth fell in love with Mary Hutchinson, who a year or two later became his wife. The track leads on and descends to the gate of Sockburn Hall. Sockburn is a peninsula: the broad silvery Tees makes a great bend south at Neasham, and below Sockburn Hall turns north again to Dinsdale and Middleton St George. This narrow, remote, southernmost peninsula of County Durham was the home of the Sockburn worm. The worm, a relation no doubt of the Lambton worm, .was slain,

according to tradition, by Sir John Conyers with the famous falchion which was always presented to every newly appointed Bishop of Durham on his entry to the Diocese, and is now in the museum at Durham Cathedral. (*See* Neasham.) The Sockburn worm, of course, is dead; 'the furious screaming of this dragon or flying fiery serpent' is heard no more. What is heard is the vociferous barking and yapping of dogs—and on approaching the tiny ruined church the visitor will be surrounded by scores of friendly dogs. Sockburn Hall is a kennels. There are dogs inside the house, dogs outside; dogs in kennels, dogs in wired pens and cages; dogs look out of the windows of the house, dogs prowl all around. The Conyers are departed too. The last baronet died a pauper in a workhouse at Chester-le-Street in 1810. Sockburn passed to the Blacketts: their arms adorn the porch of the present *Hall*, an early Victorian-Tudor house. The ruins of the *church* lie among nettles to the south, the east wall survives, with three Early English lancet windows, as does the south arcade. The north aisle, or Conyers Chapel, is roofed and glazed, and here it is possible to see the considerable collection of Anglo-Saxon fragments and Conyers monuments, in particular the effigy of a cross-legged knight, his feet resting on a monster—perhaps the great Sir John who slew the worm. A new church was built in 1838 on the Yorkshire side of the river, and Sockburn church has mouldered ever since—only the Conyers Chapel being maintained.

South Shields *see* Shields, South

Spen, High [3] Old industrial village on the high ground between Chopwell and Winlaton. The small red-brick church stands in a rural setting, in a prominent position with grand views towards Gibside across the River Derwent.

Spennymoor [10] A hundred and fifty years ago Spennymoor was a wild tract of country in the parish of Whitworth: the sinking of the coal mines, and other more recent industries, have resulted in the sprawling town that now meets the traveller on the road from Bishop Auckland to Durham. There are terraces of extraordinary red-brick Victorian houses, with lavish terracotta decoration and quasi-Byzantine arcades surmounting bay windows; on the left stands *St Paul's church* (1875) with its ogee-capped tower. The church was gutted by fire in 1953, and restored by Mr Dykes-Bower; well-furnished interior, with gaily painted chancel roof. The churchyard has been landscaped, and the gravestones banished: against the north side of the church stands a row of disgraced memorial obelisks—one with a flat round top looking like an old-fashioned pillar box. The street descends—with small shops and fish-and-chip bars—to the centre of the town, with its early 20th-century *town hall* in a diluted Baroque style. The cinemas are now dedicated to bingo: The Arcadian Bingo Hall, Lucky Seven Bingo, Collins' Prize Bingo—all compete for our patronage. Behind are vast and intimidating blocks of modern flats, like enormous human broiler houses. Beyond are two churches by Hodgson Fowler: *St Andrew's, Tudhoe Grange* (1884) in an attractive Perpendicular style; and *Holy Innocents, Tudhoe* (1866), only a short distance away, in a less sophisticated Early English idiom. A little further north is the *R.C. church*, with elaborate rose window and west porch, and spacious and lofty interior.

Springwell [4] From Gateshead the Old Durham Road climbs to High Fell and reaches Springwell—a town centre with the usual shops and supermarkets. But the road south (to Usworth) crosses a level crossing, and here is the *Bowes Railway*, now reopened as a railway museum, and the only rope railway in existence. The railway, built by George Stephenson and opened in 1826, served a string of nine collieries across a stretch of some fifteen miles, with seven rope-hauled inclines. The closure of the collieries between 1968 and 1974 brought the railway to an end—but a stretch of the track has now been reopened, and the railway restored to working order.

Staindrop [15] A long green, lined on either side with many good stone houses, leads to a narrower street towards the church: on the right is *Staindrop House*—with front door and some Jacobean windows on to the street, to which it presents a somewhat grim façade. Impressive *church*, with tall tower, the lower part Norman, the upper 14th century, wide aisles, clerestoried nave, long chancel—the exterior appears all 14th century. The first impression on entering by the south porch is of very wide aisles, Norman arcades and a sweeping vista to the transept: the interior is indeed impressive too. Above the arcades the walls of the nave are Saxon—with blocked Saxon windows. A Norman chancel arch and ancient screen (the only pre-Reformation screen in the county) leads into the chancel, resplendent with ancient stalls with misericords. At the west end of the church are the grand monuments of the Lords of Raby—Nevilles in the south-west corner, Vanes in the north-west. There is a great alabaster tomb of Ralph Neville, 1st Earl of Westmorland (d. 1425) with his two wives, and another, of blackened oak, of Henry, 5th Earl (d. 1564) and his two wives; in the opposite corner are the tombs of Henry Vane, 2nd Earl of Darlington (d. 1792), of his wife (d. 1807), of William Vane, 1st Duke of Cleveland (d. 1842), by Westmacott, and of his Duchess (d. 1859). Here and elsewhere are many later monuments to the family, and an array of hatchments. Beyond the church the road turns north and passes the long wall of Raby Park. And soon the castle comes in sight. (*See* Raby Castle.)

Stainton, Great [16] In no way great: a huddle of houses and farm buildings, and a church of 1876 (by J. P. Pritchett) with broach spire, in a large tree-lined churchyard. Wide views of unspoiled countryside north-east of Darlington.

Stanhope [8, 9] 'Capital of Weardale'. The road west from Wolsingham leads through scenery of increasing loveliness: wild moorland is all around, but the hills about Stanhope are hung with woods. A broad street leads into the square: Stanhope Castle to the west, the parish church to the north. The rich lead mines of Weardale made Stanhope a wealthy living, and there has been a long succession of eminent rectors, no less than eight of whom have become bishops, including the celebrated Bishop Butler. The *rectory* is a substantial house of 1824; a stone in the wall records the fact that its predecessor was built by William Hartwell, D.D. 'Anno pacis evangelii 1697, Ryswici 1' (In the year of the peace of the gospel 1697, the first of the Peace of Ryswick). The *church* is a plain solid building with squat tower, and incorporates work from the 12th to the 14th century; dark interior, with two Flemish baroque panels in the chancel, and a Roman altar in the vestry, found on Bollihope Common in 1747 'Silvano invicto sacrum': Silvanus was the god of the woods. By the churchyard entrance is the stump of a fossilized tree, some two hundred and fifty million years old. *Stanhope Castle*, a castellated house of 1798 (built by Cuthbert Rippon, M.P. for Gateshead) presents a rather forbidding face to the square—it is now a reform school—but a grand and

formal front to the river behind: there is a splendid walled garden, with battlemented garden house, to the west of the church. And further to the west *Stanhope Hall* is a great mediaeval hulk of a house, with one buttressed end displaying blocked early windows—the whole remodelled in the 17th century, and botched and subdivided later. *Unthank Hall*, to the south across a ford, is a 17th-century manor house, once the home of the ancient family of Maddison.

Stanley [4] Hilltop industrial town: new housing estates climb the hill on all sides, and lead up to the Victorian streets that surround the *parish church*, a rock-faced building of 1876 (by J. G. Holl) with a tall minaret between the gables at the west end; the battlemented tower with its narrow tapering spire was added to the east end in 1931, making an odd but attractive composition. The centre of the town is pedestrianized; and Nonconformist chapels abound. But the most prominent building in the town now is the enormous and extraordinary supermarket recently completed, standing alone on a central site: steps lead up to it as to a great temple, and its vast windowless upper storey is a 'Bowls Centre'—altogether a strange place of worship. Just off the road to Beamish is the *East Stanley Cemetery*; close to the gates stands the suitably sombre pink and grey granite monument to the 168 victims of the West Stanley Colliery explosion in 1909. From here and everywhere are wide views across industrial north-west Durham.

Startforth [15] Lovely position on the south bank of the Tees facing Barnard Castle: from the churchyard there is a good view of the castle and the town. The *church* is of 1863, by J. and W. Hay of Liverpool, with a low tower sprouting into an eccentric broach spire:

simple Victorian interior with modern oak seating; the 15th-century font and two 14th-century monuments in the sanctuary are reminders of its mediaeval origins. A curious obelisk in the churchyard is inscribed, 'This pedestal is raised to the memory of Hannah Latham, murdered by a sanguinary villain on the Brignall road, 1813.' To the west of the church, close to the road, is a small 17th-century *manor house* with mullioned windows and a pretty oval over the front door; just beyond, secluded in well-wooded grounds, stands a grander 18th-century house; and at the corner of a lane below is *Low Startforth Hall*, with gay chinoiserie windows.

Stella [4] A romantic-sounding name, but now only a built-up suburban stretch of housing along the main road from Gateshead to Ryton: Dunston, Blaydon, Stella follow each other; the 19th-century *parish church*, with its prominent pinnacled tower, close to the roundabout, a 20th-century power station, and spreading railway yards are now its landmarks. Past the roundabout, and close to the main road west, stands an unexpected *R.C. church* of 1832, an unusual building, a Gothic barn with lancet windows (some filled with Pugin glass) and short sanctuary—and, attached to the west end on the sloping ground, an imposing presbytery, castellated and turreted, forming a grand domestic front to the church. On the higher ground behind stood *Stella Hall*, an Elizabethan house classicized by James Paine in the 18th century, demolished in the 1950s. This was the home of the Tempest family, baronets, a recusant branch of the ancient and important Durham family (*see* Holmside and Wynyard) which received a baronetcy from James I in 1622. The daughter and heiress of the 4th baronet married the unfortunate 4th Lord Widdrington who took part in the 1715 Rebellion, and 'by this rash adventure, as by a stroke of lightning, blasted and withered a family that had for seven centuries flourished in affluence and honour'. Their title was attainted, and their rich estates in Northumberland and Lincolnshire forfeited. Francis Widdrington, however, the attainted peer's son, inherited his mother's property here, which subsequently descended to the Towneleys of Towneley, Lancashire. The only relic of this once-great house is the little octagonal gazebo, standing on a high escarpment overlooking the Tyne. The site of the mansion has been built over: Tempest Street and Widdrington Street keep alive the names of its former unfortunate owners, 'shipwrecked' as Mervyn James has remarked, 'by the burden of fine and proscription' (*Family, Lineage, and Civil Society*, Clarendon Press, 1974).

Stillington [17] Iron works. An ugly red-brick village, a sudden industrial eruption in the countryside south of Sedgefield. A flaming-red 19th-century *church* on rising ground to the east.

Stockton-on-Tees [17] The long and unexpectedly wide High Street gives the town distinction. From the river, where the bridge carries the A67 across to Thornaby and Middlesbrough, Bridge Road leads up into the High Street: in the centre stands the *Town Hall*, an elegant brick building of 1736, crowned with a little clock tower with diminutive spire; in front stands the *Market Cross*, a Tuscan column of 1756, and in front of that the *Shambles*, a local building of white brick (1825). These make a charming classical ensemble. A little further on, on the east side of the street, stands the early 18th-century *Parish Church*. Stockton is an ancient market town, but until 1711 was merely a chapelry of Norton. The church is of red brick, with

stone quoins and tripartite windows; the tower is a commanding feature of the High Street. There is some evidence that Sir Christopher Wren was consulted about its design, but it is too much to claim that he was the architect; indeed the chancel was rebuilt in 1906 in Edwardian Baroque—somewhat overpowering the nave—and a south chapel, in sympathetic 'Wrenaissance', added in 1925 by W. D. Caroe. Inside, the best feature is the 18th-century pulpit, set on tall rusticated columns. No houses of any distinction line the High Street: there has been some rebuilding, and the jazzy shopfronts are commonplace. North of the church, however, in Church Road, are a few imposing 18th-century houses with elaborate doorways (such as *72 Paradise Row*), but much of the street has been torn apart to build the new Public Library and Public Baths. For a glimpse of old Stockton it is worth visiting *Green Dragon Yard*, close to the town hall and east of the High Street. A narrow alley leads towards the river, and in the cobbled yard itself are old ramshackle warehouses and cottages, now being preserved and converted for cultural purposes. Here is some of the atmosphere of the old port of Stockton. It was the opening of the Stockton and Darlington Railway in 1825 that began the industrialization of the town, and the rapid rise in its population. The old ticket office of the S. & D. R. at *41 Bridge Street* has been reopened (to celebrate the 150th anniversary) as a museum. For the imposing late Victorian *railway station* it is necessary to turn left out of the High Street by the North Eastern Hotel: opposite the station is the *Queen's Hotel*, with its long rows of sash windows—but so much of this part of the town is depressing, with its vast areas of derelict sites. Prince Regent Street (parallel to the High Street) contains the *College of Further Education* (late Victorian

Arts and Crafts, with onion domes), and leads back towards the bridge. Here stands *Holy Trinity church*, with its decapped spire, all in blackened stone (by J. and B. Green, 1838), in its attractive setting of old churchyard and wide tree-lined green. Norton Road is the continuation north of High Street. Here are early 19th-century houses and terraces—but there has been much destruction of old property, and high-rise flats ruin the scale of the early Victorian town. *St Mary's R.C. church* is by Pugin (1841), with a somewhat sombre silhouette of stone dormer windows and attenuated tower. Just past the Fiesta Night Club we bear left for Norton, the mother parish of Stockton. Norton is a *church* of special interest on account of its rare Saxon crossing tower; it is also a building of great charm. The upper part of the tower is Perpendicular, but, below, the triangular-headed Saxon windows are at once apparent. Inside, the nave arcades are Transitional, but the eye is led at once to the venerable crossing, where the low arches to nave and chancel are Norman, and the two to the transepts Saxon. Long chancel with distinguished Early English south doorway. Under the tower an exceedingly good early 14th-century effigy of a knight in chain mail: under the cusped arch over his head are the arms of the Fulthorpe family, but his shield bears the arms of the 16th-century Sir William Blakiston: evidently the Blakistons 'borrowed' the effigy of Sir Roger Fulthorpe, and substituted their own arms. In the north transept are two 17th-century monuments to the Davisons, who succeeded the Blakistons at Blakiston (a few miles to the north-west; Fulthorpe a mile beyond that). That to Thomas Davison refers to his part in the

Doorway in Paradise Row, **Stockton-on-Tees**

Civil War, when he served 'in exercitu Regis Caroli Martyris'. An early 19th-century tablet to John Hogg describes him as 'a most amiable man of great taste in polite literature'; but his son William, a Scholar of Clare, was 'stricken with a fatal illness while studying for a university scholarship, and died aged 19'. Norton preserves the atmosphere of a distinguished, if somewhat sophisticated, village. There is a spreading green with pond and 18th-century houses and cottages lining its sides: a tree-hung street with an engaging variety of 18th-century houses and cottages connects the green with Norton

Road. In Imperial Avenue (on the east side of Norton Road) is *St Michael's*, built by Temple Moore (1912), an inexpensive but attractive church by that accomplished architect. Here and all about, great estates of council houses, built between the wars, proliferate. But beyond, surprisingly, a few green fields divide Norton from nearby Billingham.

Streatlam [15] (pronounced Streetlam) On the A688 (Barnard Castle to Staindrop) are the elegant Classical lodges and gates to Streatlam Castle: they appear late 18th century, but are in fact chaste late

Victorian reproductions. They are all that survive to remind us of the great house of the Bowes family, demolished in 1927. William Bowes, in the 15th century, rebuilt the castle—a pele tower—which was later incorporated in the great mansion built by Sir William Bowes in the early 18th century. It was three storeys high, the centre of nine bays, two-bay projecting wings on either side, and crowned by three stone cupolas. It was the principal Bowes seat (*see also* Gibside), and so remained until its sale in 1922.

Sunderland [5] Sunderland stands at the mouth of the River Wear: it is a great shipbuilding town, a port with a history stretching back to the middle ages—and earlier—and now a vast county borough which has absorbed the whole ring of villages which stood on either side of the river or along the coast to north or south. The whole town is known as Sunderland; however Sunderland itself is but the old township which stands on the south bank of the river, close to the sea (the land *sundered* from the earlier episcopal or monastic villages to the west and north). The most ancient settlement at the mouth of the river is Monkwearmouth, on the north bank, whose history goes back to the 7th century. Here we may begin our tour of Sunderland. The little *church of St Peter*, founded in 675, stands across a newly formed grass sward, in a spacious churchyard, against a background of the cranes and machinery of the shipyard. In recent years the Sunderland Corporation has cleared away the sordid surroundings of mean buildings—and there the church stands: the scene is a magic blend of antiquity and industry. The narrow tall tower at the west end dates from the 9th or 10th century, and is built on top of the 7th-century porch with its open archway, and, above the little window, the crude

Sunderland streetscape

traces of a very early sculptured figure, perhaps of St Peter or Christ in Majesty. The west wall of the nave with its steep gable is undoubtedly the earliest part of the whole building: the nave, like that at Escomb, is exceedingly lofty for its length and width. The chancel with its chancel arch is 14th century; the north aisle is a rebuilding of 1874. But the north doorway is 14th century. The founder of St Peter's was St Benedict Biscop, a young Northumbrian of noble birth who after serving at the court of the Northumbrian king entered the monastery at Lérins near Cannes, and in 669 returned to England

with Theodore of Tarsus, who had recently been consecrated Archbishop of Canterbury. In 674 the king granted him land at the mouth of the Wear, and here Benedict founded his monastery, building his church in the following year. In 681 he founded the house of St Paul at Jarrow, and the twin religious foundations of St Peter and St Paul were run as a single monastery. After the dissolution in 1536 St Peter's became a parish church; nothing remains of the monastic buildings. A new vicarage has recently been built above the north-east corner of the churchyard, and a chapter house or parish

hall added to the north-east corner of the church (1970). Here is an admirable museum, and many Saxon relics are displayed. Opposite the west front of the church stand the new buildings of the Sunderland *Boiler Makers' Social Club*, and in the main street beyond stands *Monkwearmouth station*, which with its handsome Ionic portico looks like a grand neo-classical country house. Built for George Hudson, the 'Railway King', in 1848 (architect John Dobson of Newcastle) and abandoned as a railway station, it was reopened as a museum in 1973, and is eloquent of the splendours of the early

Victorian railway age. From here it is an easy walk to the *Wearmouth Bridge*. Until the end of the 18th century the only access from Monkwearmouth to Sunderland or Bishopwearmouth was by means of ferry; in 1793 Thomas Paine (author of *The Rights of Man*) designed a bridge of cast iron for Philadelphia: the scheme came to naught, but Rowland Burdon of Castle Eden (q.v.) took the scheme over, and the bridge was built here in 1796. Robert Clarke's engraving of the bridge is dedicated to 'Rowland Burdon, Esquire, M.P., by whom this EXCELLENT PIECE of MECHANISM was invented, and under whose patronage it has been carried into execution'. The bridge was rebuilt by Stephenson in 1858 and was again rebuilt in 1929. South of the river turn left into High Street East. Here there are a few Georgian houses, and the old Exchange (now the Strand Tombola Hall), and at the bottom (bearing right) we reach the Old Town, the docks, and the parish church. Here is all the atmosphere of an old seaport—cranes and shipping tower above us; there has been much clearance of slum property, and there are great empty spaces. A street leads past *Emmaus House*—an outpost of Mirfield, run by the Community of the Resurrection—into *Trafalgar Square*, an old Merchant Seamen's Almshouse built round three sides of an open square. 'ENGLAND EXPECTS ...' reads the inscription, 'erected by the Trustees of the Muster Roll under the IVth and Vth of William IV, Anno Domini 1840.' Above are the arms of Lord Nelson. In the centre of the square is an iron urn, converted into a gas light. Further on is the old parish *school*, DONISTON SCHOOL 1827, and opposite the new parish school, a curious modern building like a collection of mustard pots—and so into Church Street. The north side of the *parish church*, with its big Georgian windows, is on our left: St Patrick's

R.C. Church in Victorian Gothic, with a tall adjacent presbytery, opposite. The parish church was built in 1719, and with its bold Baroque west tower, its ample stone quoins and dressings, its mellow red brick, its Tuscan pilasters and rusticated doorway, is decidedly handsome. The interior is spacious, the sunlight pouring in through the great windows with their clear glass; the sanctuary is an almost circular apse (an addition of 1735) with Venetian window, entered by a grand Baroque reredos-screen of plaster, adorned with cherubs and mitres and a bible. At the west end is a capacious gallery, approached by elegant staircases: painted cherubs' heads adorn the entrance from the vestibule. 'O how amiable are Thy dwellings', runs the text round the door—and inside are stalls marked CHURCH WARDEN, SIDESMAN, OVERSEER, CONSTABLE. The gallery is adorned with the Royal Arms, and cartouches of the arms of Bishop Lord Crewe and the Bishop of London. Leading off the gallery in the south-west corner is a reading room, fitted with contemporary bookshelves and writing desk. There are other good furnishings—such as the font, with its exceedingly pretty cover with dove and cherubs' heads, and the elegant communion rails. By the west door is a splendid monument by Chantry, with life-size figure, to Robert Grey, Rector of Sunderland (died 1838). The whole church is redolent of the atmosphere of the 18th century, with its ideals of good order and modest piety. The Old Town is quiet and remote; there is a background of tower blocks, a foreground of empty spaces, where little streets have been demolished wholesale. Moving west we find many surviving streets of the early 19th-century town: Villiers Street contains the chaste classical façade of the *Presbyterian chapel* (1825); Borough Street, Foyle Street and

Athenaeum Street all contain fine houses of 1820–30; Frederick Street, smaller houses. There is a long narrow square called (rather oddly) Sunniside, with more late-Georgian houses—one called the *Manor House*—and the Edwardian *post office*. And now we are in the centre of the modern town. Borough Road borders Mowbray Park (with its *statues of Jack Crawford*, hero of Camperdown, and *Sir Henry Havelock*, hero of the Indian Mutiny—both natives of the town) and here is the *Public Library and Museum*, an imposing block of 1879 by the Victorian architect Tittman. Fawcett Street is the main shopping street, and leads back to High Street. In High Street West are newer shops: farther down are the *Public Baths*—Victorian Jacobean with plenty of strapwork decoration—and the Edwardian *police station* by T. R. Milburn. And where the street turns are two more imposing Edwardian monuments: the *Empire Theatre* (1908) and, on the opposite corner, the *Dun Cow*, both by T. R. Milburn, both Baroque with domed circular towers facing each other on their corner sites. Now we are in Bishopwearmouth. The *parish church* stands to the south of the High Street, facing what was the old village green: there is a view across towards the old hospital (with its sash windows and gabled wings), now part of the teacher training college. To the east stands the vast glass and steel palace called the Sports Centre. Bishopwearmouth church from the outside appears unremarkable, with its 18th-century tower and large mid-19th-century transepts: the interior is indeed most remarkable. In fact the church was practically rebuilt in 1933 by W. D. Caroe. Transforming the transepts, and preserving the west tower, he built a new nave and chancel in his own free Perpendicular style. The nave has double aisles; there are wide vistas everywhere and stone staircases lead up to galleries; the arcades are richly detailed; there are beautiful oak pews, and the roof throughout (even in the Victorian transepts) is of the finest pale oak—indeed all the furnishings are of the highest order. There are many 18th- and 19th-century monuments in the outer aisles, transferred from the old church, including a Victorian brass to William Paley (Paley's *Evidences*), 'Bishopwearmouth's most illustrious rector'. It is a church in which it is necessary to sit and gaze about, to absorb all the details. One of the great surprises and pleasures of Sunderland is the great mid-Victorian leafy suburb of Ashbrook. This lies south of the railway line to Durham, and may be approached by Stockton Road or Burdon Road. Here in the 1860s, on the site of older mansions which stood in their own extensive grounds, elegant terraces were built in a late-Georgian style: Thornhill Terrace, Ashbrook Vale, the Avenue, the Esplanade—some in leafy streets, some in their own private enclaves—containing houses for the professional classes. There are some larger houses, several more modest terraces; Langham Tower is a great 'Elizabethan' industrialist's mansion: Alice Street contains sweet little artisans' dwellings. There are churches: in Ryhope Road is *Christ Church*, a building of 1862 by James Murray, containing Morris glass, and *St George's Presbyterian church* in Ashburne Street, a most original affair by J. P. Pritchett (1890) in red brick, with an immensely tall tower crowned by a pinnacled pyramid roof, the upper part completely open, with tall lancet windows. From here it is worth driving further south to Tunstall Hills. For those who have the energy to climb the grassy slopes there is a most rewarding view—to the harbour to the north, to Seaham and Silksworth to the south, to leafy Ashbrook below, and the blue (or grey) North Sea to the east. One more

St Andrew's Roker (*see* **Sunderland**)

church should be visited in this part of the town: *St Ignatius's, Hendon*. Built in 1889 by Hodgson Fowler, the exterior is not interesting—but the interior is rewarding. The lofty nave leads to an equally lofty, spacious chancel, to a High Altar with towering reredos. It is the kind of church which brings you to your knees. Retracing our steps towards Wearmouth Bridge, it is possible to visit the new *town hall and civic centre* in Burdon Road. Designed by Sir Basil Spence and opened in 1970, this great civic palace is built in buff-coloured brick in the form of two interlocking hexagons. It is a great fortress block of offices, with Council Chamber and Civic Suite: for the visitor the most impressive thing is the amphitheatre of steps and ramps leading up and up to the main entrance courtyard. Burdon Road leads back to Fawcett Street, and so to Bridge Street. At the corner of High Street is an incredible building in 'Hindoo Gothic': elephants emerge from under

Gothic canopies; ogee Gothick windows adorn the first floor; and among the gothic gables an Indian minaret crowns the projecting Gothic window at the corner. Closer to the bridge is *St Mary's R.C. church* in restrained and orthodox Gothic of 1835. Crossing the bridge once more, the road west (Southwick Road) commands a view of the winding River Wear, with its docks and shipyards; to the north of the road, and lost in a maze of humble streets, stands one more remarkable church: *St Columba's, Southwick*. A red-brick basilica of 1885 (by Hodgson Fowler), the interior with its long simple Byzantine arcades, apsidal sanctuary and apsidal narthex, its altars and murals and marble ornament, is solemn and devout: a numinous, imposing church for a drab, poor parish. But the road east, Roker Avenue, leads to seaside Sunderland. Terraces of hotels and boarding houses face the sea—cafés and kiosks and all the trappings of a seaside resort. Here

St Andrew's Roker (*see* **Sunderland**): the sanctuary ceiling and the south transept window

Tanfield Hall

in Roker is Sunderland's final surprise and final glory: *St Andrew's church*. Built in 1906–7 by E. S. Prior of rough-hewn local stone, the church is justly celebrated as the 'cathedral of the Arts and Crafts Movement'. It is a building of the greatest originality, Gothic-inspired but following Gothic

ideals only in spirit. Like a great cliff, it stands erect and noble among commonplace suburban seaside houses: a dominating tower at the east crossing, shallow transepts, still shallower chancel, long massive nave. Inside it resembles a ship upturned: great arches of the same rough-hewn stone span the

nave, with the narrowest of aisles as it were cut through the solid masonry at their base—the eye is carried on and up to the narrower sanctuary beyond the choir. A Burne-Jones tapestry (by Morris & Co.), an east window by Payne, altar ornaments by Gimson—such are the decorations of the east end.

176

Tow Law ▷

Ushaw College

Choir stalls, organ gallery, pulpit, all by Gimson, provide the setting. The lectern, inlaid with ebony and metal, is also Gimson's work, the font by Randal Wells. At the west end a tablet by Eric Gill records the dedication 'in memory of Janet Priestman by her children': everything is in harmony, the church a masterpiece.

Tanfield [4] Rough country north of Stanley: old collieries around, and an industrial estate in the valley below. But the village is small and unexpectedly secluded. The *church* is substantially of 1749; tower and chancel were rebuilt in the 19th century. There is a marble floor-slab to Sir William Wray of Beamish (1628) with touching verse—the Wrays of Beamish descended from a brother of Sir Christopher Wray, Queen

Elizabeth's Lord Chief Justice, of Glentworth in Lincolnshire; and a marble monument to Dorothea Methold (1857), daughter of Sir John Eden, 4th Bt., whose son inherited the Beamish estate (q.v.). East of the church is *Tanfield Hall*, with its tall simple early 18th-century façade masking an earlier core. In front is a remarkable iron screen, with astonishingly elaborate iron gates leading from the walled front garden down to the road. A remarkable sight in unsophisticated Tanfield.

Thornley [11] A large village, which once served the local colliery: the colliery is closed, the mine extinct, and there are great open spaces where terraces of miners' houses have been destroyed. The *church* is of 1843, a low-gabled, aisleless, ecclesiastical box, with a bell-

cote. Opposite stands the shell of the Ritz Cinema—derelict. Little *R.C. church* with wooden-traceried windows.

Thorpe Thewles [17] The great railway viaduct, which carried the line from Stockton to Sunderland, stands abruptly terminated where the new dual carriageway of the Stockton–Durham road (A177) roars by beneath the embankment; the line is closed, the village bypassed. Small stone *church* with bellcote and lancet windows. Two handsome public houses: the *Vane Arms*, 17th century with shapely gable; the *Hamilton-Russell Arms*, larger and plainer 18th century.

Toronto [10] (near Bishop Auckland) Of course not far from Quebec: Toronto is a little village on the A689, where the road

178

descends to the River Wear, and so to Bishop Auckland. Humble little *church* of 1903.

Tow Law [9] Long straggling streets climb the hill: terraces of grim cottages, larger houses, chapels, shops—but there is open country behind, and wide views over the surrounding district, towards Weardale to the south, and across to moorland to the west and north. Tow Law is the meeting place of many roads, to Lanchester, to Consett, to Wolsingham and to Bishop Auckland. The iron industry, and collieries, made Tow Law; now, apart from a little opencast mining, the collieries are finished, and the iron industry is finished. The *church*, by Hodgson Fowler, the Durham architect, is a building of 1869, and of some distinction: long lofty aisleless nave and chancel, with scholarly details as befits that architect. The screen—designed and executed by the incumbent, the Revd Thomas Espin (1888–1934), an amateur astronomer—a remarkable confection of fir cones and acorns and chestnuts and walnuts fastened to the framework: the effect is surprisingly successful and unusual. Church and vicarage stand together in a bleak spot at the end of a side road, close to a defunct railway line and goods yard.

Trimdon [11] Wide village street, mounting the low hill; set on a grassy mound in the middle is the little *church*, humble mediaeval—nave, chancel, bell-cote. Intimate, devout interior with Norman chancel arch. Victorian north aisle. Two miles north of Trimdon is the colliery village, with the usual shabby Victorian streets, and a red-brick *church* surmounted by an unusual lantern-like cupola.

Ushaw College [10] The great Roman Catholic seminary stands stern but magnificent on high ground about four miles west of Durham, on the lesser road to Lanchester. It was established here in 1808—but is in fact the historic English College of Douai, which had been founded there by Cardinal Allen in 1568, to train English priests for the reconversion of England, and to educate the boys of English Roman Catholic families who were debarred from a Catholic education in England. Expelled from France in 1798, after the Revolution, the members of Douai returned to England, re-established the college first at Crook Hall (near Stanley)—a house now demolished—and then at Pontop Hall (*see* Dipton), and finally came to Ushaw in 1808. The original building is the large Georgian block (dated 1812) which stands austere and impressive, four storeys high, fifteen bays wide, its central pediment now submerged in the later top storey. Behind this two lower wings running north formed a courtyard, later enclosed on the north side by a Gothic range, and at this time the side ranges were also gothicized. A. W. N. Pugin built the Chapel to the west of the main front (1840), which was subsequently enlarged and rebuilt by Hansom (1885); Hansom also designed the *Library* to balance it on the east. The *Refectory* (Pugin) lies behind the court, as does a Hall, known as the *Exhibition Room* (Hansom). Around and behind is a great labyrinth of further wings and courts of many dates, and a new modern *Study Block* quite recently completed. And further to the west and almost independent are the *school buildings* (by E. W. Pugin, 1857), with another open quadrangle, and its own chapel. Since 1975 the school has been moved to the sister establishment at Upholland in Lancashire. The most spectacular building is the *College Chapel*, entered by a spacious antechapel. Much of the glass and many of the fittings are by Pugin (from the earlier chapel), and there are many smaller chapels around, lavishly decorated, and redolent of Catholic piety. Indeed the whole college is redolent of that synthesis of austerity and devotion which one associates with the Roman Catholic revival in 19th-century England. Along the boundary of the playing field to the east are what appear to be brick fortifications enclosing low covered courts—where the traditional Ushaw game, imported from Douai, is played. Bordering the road to the west stand enormously tall and impressive farm buildings by Hansom (1852). The college is open to visitors by prior arrangement with the President's secretary.

Ushaw Moor [10] (south of Ushaw College) Not a moor at all—but a humble little industrial village in the valley of the Deerness below Ushaw College. Little red-brick basilica *church* of 1914.

Usworth [4] On the edge of Washington New Town: new roads, new factories, new estates. The older village is round the blackened stone *church* (1842) by John Green. *Usworth Hall*, a plain Georgian villa of 1830, is now headquarters of the Washington Development Corporation.

Walworth [16] Walworth Castle stands against rising countryside north of the Tees: from the south it is visible for miles—caught in sunlight, perhaps—from the Roman road to Piercebridge. The house was built by Thomas Jennison, Auditor-General in Ireland, c. 1600. The south front is three storeys high, with a round tower at each end: lower wings behind enclose a courtyard where a spectacular centrepiece at the back of the main front formed the original entrance, with coupled columns, Doric on the ground floor, Ionic on the first and Corinthian on the second, and a balustraded parapet at the top. This is reminiscent of the Bodleian Library or Merton College at Oxford, Lyme Hall in Cheshire or Browsholme in

Walworth Castle

Yorkshire, as the round towers are reminiscent of Lulworth in Dorset. Sash windows replaced some of original mullions on the courtyard side, and the courtyard was in the 19th century enclosed on the north side. King James I stayed here on his first entrance to England in 1603. Walworth subsequently passed through various families—Stephensons, Harrisons and finally Aylmers (monuments in Heighington church): it is now a Durham County Council special school.

Washington [4] The New Town of Washington was first proposed in 1964: unemployment in the northeast was high, and the old collieries in the district were closing; the object was to attract new industries to the area—and to provide for an eventual population of some 80,000. A master plan was produced, and work on the New Town began in 1967. Building is still in progress. There is a nucleus of old village round the church, and signposts with the Stars and Stripes direct the traveller to Washington Old Hall. The church stands on rising ground; it is chiefly of 1833—replacing a mediaeval building—and was built by the rector, Henry Percival, who was the son of the Prime Minister who had the misfortune to be murdered (in 1812). The church was enlarged once or twice in the next century, and the little bell turret was added in 1962. The only thing surviving from the old church is the font: above it hang the Stars and Stripes. *Washington Old Hall* stands immediately to the south of the church—more Stars and Stripes!—and is a delightful early 17th-century manor house: two gables face the church, three face south, with a more pronounced E-plan on that front, the central gable containing the front door and staircase. The Washington family indeed take their name from Washington—a matter of pride for County Durham—and came to live here (from Hartburn near Stockton) at the end of the 12th century. Sir Walter Washington (mid-13th century) had three sons. George

180

Washington was descended from the third, and his ancestors migrated to Lancashire, and so to Sulgrave in Northamptonshire, whence they emigrated to America. Descendants of the two elder sons inherited Washington, and the male line ended in the early 15th century. Descendants in the female line sold the place to Bishop James of Durham in 1612: it was he or his son who built the present house. By the early 1950s this was derelict and decaying, and threatened with demolition—when a public-spirited group of local people rallied round, bought the place, restored it, and presented it to the National Trust. The hall, by which we enter, is a characteristic room of its period, paved with stone flags, and with a low beamed ceiling. Of special interest are the two Gothic arches into the kitchen, which survive from the mediaeval house of the Washingtons. There is an oak-panelled room at the east end, with good contemporary panelling from a house in Hertfordshire. The Jacobean staircase came from the White Hart at Guildford, and was presented by Lord Gort (*see* Hamsterley). There is appropriate furniture throughout the house, and friends on both sides of the Atlantic have rallied round to equip and endow the place. Much is made of the connection with George Washington, and the house is often referred to as the 'ancestral home of George Washington'—perhaps a slight exaggeration, as his last direct ancestor to live here died in the 13th century, and only the kitchen wall with the Gothic arches can date back to those days. However, as a Jacobean manor house it is well worth a visit, in its own right: its remarkable rescue in our own times is a triumph. There is also an interesting collection of souvenirs of the great man. A native of Washington who should be honoured is Gertrude Bell: daughter of Sir Thomas Hugh Bell, and granddaughter of Sir Isaac

Washington Old Hall

Lowthian Bell, one of the founders of Middlesbrough, she was born at Washington Hall in 1868. *Washington Hall* stands a short distance from the Old Hall, and was built by Gertrude's grandfather in 1854; the architect was A. B. Higham. Gabled, turreted and pinnacled, of red brick decorated with black diapers, it is a building of some Victorian distinction. Inside, a plaque records 'Gertrude Bell: Scholar, Historian, Archaeologist, Explorer, Poet, Mountaineer, Gardener, Distinguished servant of the State: Born here, 14 July 1868, died Baghdad, 12 July 1926'. The house is now a school for deprived children. Washington was for two

hundred years surrounded by coal mines: the 'F' pit shaft was sunk in 1777, and so was one of the oldest working pits in the country when it closed in 1968. Harraton, Glebe and Usworth mines have also now closed, but the winder house and steam engine of Washington 'F' have been preserved, and opened as part of an industrial museum devoted to mining. The *'F' Pit Museum* may be found by the A1231, turning off at Windlass Lane. The great slag heap, which once dominated the landscape, has been removed, and the materials used to build the new roads for the New Town. From the A1 (M) it is possible to see something of the

New Town. Large signposts appear, directing the visitor to 'District 5' or 'District 6'—which at first seem somewhat intimidating. In fact the New Town is conceived as a series of villages planned on a pleasant domestic scale, with industrial estates widely dispersed in different areas. There are shops and offices at the centre of the town: the various villages are grouped all round—some old villages which have become engulfed, others being given appropriate or local names. Old defunct collieries and acres and acres of derelict sites have been landscaped and planted with trees, and the villages are built around their greens in suitable Durham fashion, with local shops and village halls. All the planning has been in the hands of the Architectural Department of the Corporation, and many of the schemes have won awards from the Department of the Environment. There is Sulgrave, and there is Columbia, Harraton, Lambton and Glebe—each with individual architectural character, and old buildings, where possible, made use of. In the words of the Chairman of the Corporation (Sir James Steel), 'We have preserved every possible hedge and tree ... we have saved streams and ponds from death by pollution: we have cleared away thousands of tons of industrial dereliction.' A village which awaits development in the next year or so is named Ayton, after the family (*see* Houghton-le-Spring) who owned the mines here. In the early 18th century, on the death of Samuel Ayton (1725), the property descended to his three daughters, one the wife of Sir Francis Blake, 1st Bt of Twizell, Northumberland, one the wife of Sir Ralph Milbanke, 5th Bt of Halnaby, Yorkshire, one the wife of Sir John Thorold, 8th Bt of Marston, Lincolnshire; they held the estate in undivided shares, and jointly worked the pits. 'From these three titled proprietors the Ayton estates have been generally named The

Three Baronets' Lands', wrote Surtees in 1820. Sir Francis Blake was the mathematician and Fellow of the Royal Society; Sir John Thorold was a Fellow of Lincoln College, Oxford, and friend of John Wesley; Sir Ralph Milbanke's daughter Elizabeth married Lord Melbourne, father of the Prime Minister, and his granddaughter Annabella married Lord Byron (*see* Seaham). On a map of 1801 the individual pits are marked: one is called the *Blake*, one the *Milbanke*, one the *Thorold*, another the *Melbourne*, another the *Annabella*. So the new village will recall a short episode of local history, and a long-forgotten name.

West Boldon *see* Boldon

West Rainton *see* Rainton

Westerton [10] Hilltop hamlet: on the green stands the odd little Gothic *Observatory tower* built by Thomas Wright of Byers Green (q.v.) c. 1770. Wide views on all sides—over Auckland Park, the colliery village of Coundon and the surrounding countryside.

Westgate [8] Beyond Eastgate, of course, on the long lonely road through Weardale: with every mile the landscape becomes wilder. The disused railway track accompanies the road and the river: there is a street of stone houses and cottages—with a prominent clock over the road; small apsidal *church* with bellcote by Withers (1869).

Wheatley Hill [11] A tragic run-down mining village, which served the (now extinct) collieries of the East Durham coalfield: run-down streets with a few shops—the Regal Cinema (closed)—a grand little domed building in the High Street, marked 'Boot Dept'—a little brick church of 1914. Side streets lead off to nowhere. But newer council houses near the main road (one street is named Jack Lawson Terrace, in honour of the miners' leader who became Lord Lawson, and Lord Lieutenant of the

County) are more prosperous, and new industries are being imported.

Whickham [4] A built-up village of well-to-do 'commuter' houses on the crest of the hills above the Tyne: shops and banks, a prosperous public house, council offices and a few older houses occupy the main street; and the *church* lies back overlooking Church Green. A sturdy 13th-century west tower, Norman chancel arch, Transitional south arcade; the north arcade and two north aisles are Victorian additions built to enlarge the church as the population of the village grew; ornate 19th-century reredos and east end. A brass plate at the west end records the restoration of the church under Salvin in 1862, and a marble tablet in the chancel commemorates Henry Byrne Carr, rector for fifty years (1846–96): 'Under him and largely through his liberality the old parish church was restored, new churches built at Marley Hill and Dunston, and lastly at Swalwell, the Church Green saved, the church schools restored and maintained, and anxious times of cholera and destitution overcome.' There are also some handsome earlier monuments: to Dr Thomlinson, Prebendary of St Paul's and rector (d. 1747) on north side of the sanctuary; to the Revd William Williamson (1763), and John Carr, Esq. (1817) on the south side, both signed by Jopley, sculptor of Gateshead; and in a spandrel of the south arcade a chaste little tablet to Anthony Leaton, Arm^r of Whickham House (1803), with a shield of arms on a little marble urn. Close to the south door is another 18th-century monument, to Sir James Clavering of Axwell and to his son Sir Thomas, 'Member of Parliament in four successive parliaments', (1794). In the churchyard is a memorial (erected 1891) to William Shield, the composer, born here in 1748, who became Director of Covent Garden and Master of the King's Musick. A few houses call for special mention: the former *rectory*, now the Cottage Hospital, stands south-west of the church, a dignified stone building of 1713, with a spirited coat of arms of Lord Crewe, Bishop of Durham, in the pediment of the front door; and a mile south on the road towards the Team Valley Trading Estate, *Dunston Hill*, a mansion of 1743, with a grand, plain façade—once the home of the Carrs and Carr-Ellisons, but now a hospital, its front mutilated by incongruous appendages. And at the east end of the church is Park Cottage, an amusing Georgian Gothick archway, converted into a house. (For Axwell Park, *see* Blaydon.)

Whitburn [5] On the coast north of Sunderland, a pretty, if sophisticated, village, an unexpected oasis, which owes its appearance and its survival to the Williamsons, baronets, who were seated here from the early 18th century until the 20th. The 1st baronet was of East Markham, Nottinghamshire; the 2nd married a Fenwick, heiress of Monkwearmouth, the 4th a Hedworth, heiress of Harraton, who brought the family still greater Durham wealth and influence. Every holder of the title since has been christened Hedworth: the 7th and 8th baronets were M.P.s for the County or for Sunderland. *Whitburn Hall*, their former home, stands behind its wall close to the green, a long, rambling house of many dates, with sash and oeil-de-boeuf windows, pulled together by a balustraded parapet with decorative statuary at the centre. To the south-west of the Hall in its own walled garden stands the former *rectory*, an impressive stone bow-fronted house of 1818. The *church* with its narrow buttressed tower, crowned with a low lead spire, is chiefly 13th century: long low nave and chancel, and wide aisles. There is an engaging recumbent effigy of Michael Mathew of Cleadon

(1689) with periwigged head. To the south of the church is a red-brick and terracotta Gothic cottage, and, overlooking the green, a fanciful half-timbered black and white house of 1859, an extraordinary and attractive confection.

Whitworth [10] Yet another remarkable oasis: the road north from Spennymoor (unsignposted) suddenly becomes a country lane and after some meandering reaches Whitworth—a park, a herd of deer, a tiny church and the Hall, home of the Shafto family. The Shaftos originated in Northumberland and descend from Mark Shafto, Mayor of Newcastle in 1549; they purchased Whitworth in 1652. Five generations of M.P.s for the city of Durham include Robert Shafto, the 'Bonnie Bobbie Shafto' of the song, who was Member for Durham 1760–68 and subsequently for the borough of Downton, Wiltshire. The 18th-century house was burnt in 1892; the present house is in fact the north wing, embellished and enlarged after the fire. The imposing early 19th-century library survives as an almost independent pavilion. The little *church* is of 1850, with a prettily decorated interior. There are two mediaeval effigies from the old church, curiously built into the outside west wall, and inside are various memorials to the Shaftos. The lane leads on, crosses the River Wear, and makes for Brancepeth.

Whorlton [15] Terraces of small cottages, and other houses set in gay gardens, around a spacious oblong green; in one corner stands the *Hall*—a tall, attractive, austere house of solid Victorian features, set in a garden of conifers and wellingtonias—home of the Headlams, a distinguished academic and ancient Durham family (*see* Headlam). And next to it, the *church*, modest and intimate, of 1853—filled with richly-coloured

19th-century glass. Memorials in churchyard to Headlams, notably to Arthur Cayley Headlam, C.H., Bishop of Gloucester and Fellow of All Souls. The road descends by a sharp hairpin bend to a suspension bridge (of 1829) across the River Tees, to Wycliffe. It is delectable country. Along the minor road to Barnard Castle—to the north-west of the village—is *Sledwich Hall*, a long low Elizabethan stone house, built on an H-plan but incorporating an older structure; the house was considerably restored early this century.

Willington [10] A typical small colliery town, on the A690 from Durham to Wolsingham: the rows and rows of miners' cottages, back to back, street to street, testify to the sudden growth of a small village in the mid-19th century. The population in 1801 was 164: by 1861 it was 2,393. Cottages were quickly run up to house the miners in Willington Colliery to the south, Brancepeth Colliery to the north. The *church* stands at the east end of the village, a stone Perpendicular church of 1858 by J. A. Cory, with west tower crowned by low pyramid. Well-furnished Victorian interior with handsome pews and colourful east window. Opposite stands a solid Victorian rectory: on the west side a Gothick house, stuccoed and now somewhat tatty, with pretty windows and battlements. To the south the River Wear winds its way: the by-road to Binchester provides a glimpse of the Old Hall, a tall, rustic, ancient house which has seen better days, and leads to Newfield, where there is the battered fragment of another ancient house, with mullioned windows—now derelict. Another road (B6296) to Helmington and Hunwick leads to another, specially gloomy, suburb called (à la Durham humour) Sunnybrow, where there is a large red-brick church of 1889—now closed. A sad spot.

183

Wingate [11] Large colliery village: terraces of glum-faced brick cottages climb the slowly rising hill; mutilated countryside around. Early Victorian stone *church*, wide and low, by G. L. Jackson of Durham (1840).

Winlaton [4] Old industrial built-up countryside above the Tyne: village setting for church and dignified stone rectory. The *church* is an attractive building of 1828, by Ignatius Bonomi, with solid west tower and lofty-aisled nave and short chancel, all in an early Perpendicular revival style—very different from Bonomi's later churches. Churchyard of old tombstones and fine trees.

Winston [15] The delectable country of the Tees valley: the river runs down its rocky course between steep and verdant banks, and is crossed in one great span (111 feet) by a *bridge* designed by Sir Thomas Robinson (of Rokeby, q.v.) in 1764. The *church*, simple and austere with its bell turret, stands above the river at the end of the village: partly rebuilt in the 19th century, the chancel with its narrow lancet windows is ancient, as is the nave arcade. Remarkable font with carved dragons in conflict, perhaps 14th century; two small brass inscriptions (15th and 16th centuries), and one (early 17th century) to Dowthwaites of Westholme. *Westholme* stands a mile north, just off the B6274, an early 17th-century manor house built on an H-plan, with gables and mullioned windows. It was built by John Dowthwaite, who married a Scrope, and so was a recusant house. The garden descends with formal hedges below the south front; it is an altogether delightful smaller squire's house. And a mile or two west of the village, along the A67, but deeply hidden down a long drive, stands *Stubb House*, a tall and handsome stone house of 1750, with low pedimented pavilion

wings of 1816 on either side of the south front. It is now a county council school.

Witton Gilbert [10] (pronounced with a soft 'g'). The main street is of the usual hard, glum, Durham complexion: to the south a lane leads off to the church and Witton Hall. The *church*, with its double bellcote, was much rebuilt in 1863, but there is Norman work in the chancel and south side of the nave; inside it is whitewashed and charming with High Church ornaments. Nearby, the *Hall* retains a few fragments of the mediaeval leper hospital, including a 13th-century window. And the lane leads down to the little River Browney, sequestered and leafy—for all the proximity of the defunct colliery at Langley Park opposite. The main road (A691) leads on to Lanchester; a mile beyond the village a minor road forks right and climbs the hill towards Burnhope. Here in the darkest of dark woodlands stand the crumbling remains of *Langley Hall*, built in the 16th century by Henry, Lord Scrope of Bolton and his wife, a Dacre of Greystoke. In the 17th century it passed by marriage to the 5th Marquis of Winchester, who was created Duke of Bolton; but his descendants sold it in the 18th century—and it has crumbled ever since. It was in origin a courtyard house, but there is little left to tell the tale.

Witton-le-Wear [9] For all the proximity of Witton Park, that depressed and depressing broken-down 19th-century industrial village, Witton-le-Wear is a village of some character and antiquity. The streets are built on the edge of rising ground; above the narrow green is the church; and streets both below and above the green have buildings of some interest. A house in the lower street has an odd Gothicky tower with conical top; at the end of the upper street stands Witton

Tower, a pele tower, refaced in the 17th century, attached to the remains of a mediaeval manor house. The small *church* has a 13th-century north arcade, but was otherwise rebuilt by Hodgson Fowler in 1902. South-east of the village in its park stands *Witton Castle*, which was originally built in the early 14th century by Sir Ralph Eure. The keep, or north-east tower, is original, as is the imposing curtain wall with its angle towers. The castle was greatly added to in succeeding centuries, with the ample domestic quarters stretching on and on round a further courtyard—and much was rebuilt and glorified in mediaeval fashion in the 19th; but it is without question a romantic and splendid *tout ensemble*. From the Eures it passed to the Darcys, Cuthberts, Hoppers and finally, in the 19th century, to the Chaytors, baronets, who remained in possession till after the second war. It now belongs to Lord Lambton, and is run as a kind of holiday camp, with bars in the dungeon, dining rooms in the keep, and recreation rooms elsewhere. The park is full of caravans, the courtyard full of cars, the gardens full of campers—so the spirit of the place is lost. It is, however, some compensation that the place survives, and is used.

Wolsingham [9] (pronounced Woolsingham) A somewhat dour little town in Weardale with steel works; but these do not obtrude unduly, and the middle of the town has some austere charm. *Whitfield House* is a tall early 18th-century house, with parapet and quoins, six bays of sash windows, and three storeys. It stands dignified and a little withdrawn behind a pair of ilex trees, which give it a slightly French air. Next door *Whitfield Place* is dated 1677; it is long and low

Whitburn (*top*)

Witton-le-Wear ▷

184

with mullioned and two bay windows. Of the parish *church* the tower is 12th century—the rest rebuilt in Early English style by Moffatt and Scott (1848), and typical of their early work. Next door is the early 19th-century stone vicarage. Large and spacious *R.C. church* by Hansom (1854). East of the town, and close to the main road, stands *Bradley Hall*, in origin mediaeval, but substantially transformed into a farmhouse in the 18th century.

Wolviston [11] Traffic rushes by on the A689—east to west—and on the dual carriageway of the A19—north to south. But both roads bypass the village. There are a number of worthwhile cottages and larger houses in the interlocking streets, and round the green: the old *Parochial School* (1836) has pretty Gothic windows and is now a private house; the *Ship Inn* is bright red Victorian. The *church* with its flèche is of 1876 (by Austin Johnson and Hicks): a new church hall has been added to the north side of the building (1972). Across the churchyard is a charming little *Methodist chapel* with Georgian features and round-headed windows (1829).

Wycliffe [15] (pronounced Wycliffe) An idyllic spot on the River Tees. A narrow lane leads off a minor road, down to the church and (former) rectory, a dignified Georgian house with projecting wings. The *church* is a sturdy, simple, rustic 13th–14th-century building with bellcote and south porch: well-furnished interior—with interesting roof of 1963 by William Whitfield, composed of coffered lozenges, the chancel gaily painted. Much mediaeval stained glass in south windows, and several small monuments and inscriptions to the Wycliffe family: according to tradition, John Wycliffe, 'morning star of the Reformation', was born here. *Wycliffe Hall* stands above the River Tees on higher ground to the east, a distinguished stone house of

Wycliffe Roman Catholic church

Wycliffe parish church

186

c. 1750, with three-storeyed centrepiece and lower, slightly projecting, wings either side: spreading lawns and splendid trees provide a perfect setting; facing the house is a dovecote with stone pyramid roof by William Whitfield (1955). Long wings behind the house conceal portions of the earlier manor house: one room may be mediaeval and date back to the time of John Wycliffe. Some of the interior was gutted by fire thirty years ago, but was excellently restored with plaster ceilings from Halnaby, the Milbanke house near Croft (*see* Hurworth). A large room on the first floor in the west wing is of c. 1800, and may have been the Roman Catholic Chapel. The recusant family of Tunstall, who succeeded the Wycliffes in the 17th century, inherited in 1721 the great house of Burton Constable in the E. Riding, and became in course of time Constables, and Clifford-Constables, and finally Chichester-Constables. Wycliffe became subsidiary to the great Yorkshire estate, and in the 19th century was let for long periods—one of the tenants being the author's great-great-grandfather. In an exposed position on the road to Hutton Magna stands the Roman Catholic church, built in 1848, a Gothic barn with one window by Wailes, and a priest's house and school attached. There are sweeping views across this high exhilarating country from the churchyard.

Wynyard [11] Although only a few miles from Hartlepool, Billingham and Stockton, Wynyard stands in its own secluded park: for all the proximity of industry, thick woods and farmland surround it, and only a glimpse of a tall obelisk above the trees reveals the presence of a great house here. Langtons, Conyers, Claxtons, were the owners of this manor with its private chapel in the middle ages; in 1630 it was purchased by a Newcastle merchant, Alexander Davidson, whose descendants lived here for a century. In 1742 it was purchased by John Tempest of Old Durham, M.P. for Durham: it is his descendant, Lord Londonderry, who lives here today. John Tempest's granddaughter married Sir Henry Vane of Long Newton (q.v.): their son became Sir Henry Vane-Tempest, M.P. for Durham, and it was his daughter, the redoubtable Frances Anne, who married Charles Stewart, younger son of the 1st Marquis of Londonderry and half-brother of the statesman Lord Castlereagh, whom he succeeded as 3rd Marquis in 1822. The family assumed the name of Vane-Tempest-Stewart: it is Frances Anne's great-great-great-grandson, the 9th Marquis, who lives here now. Winding drives lead to the Lion Bridge which crosses the Beck, and so to the great porticoed front. The present house was begun in 1822, and the architect was Philip Wyatt, James Wyatt's youngest son. In 1841 it was gutted by fire, and rebuilt under the supervision of Ignatius Bonomi and John Dobson on almost identical lines. The house is on the grandest scale: the long entrance front has as its centrepiece a great six-column Corinthian portico: a balustraded parapet holds the long façade together. The garden front is of equal length, with a wide bow window at each end. The rooms are large and sumptuous: the *entrance hall* leads into the *Statue Gallery*, a great domed room, which leads to the long suite of State Rooms overlooking the gardens. In the *Mirror Room* is a plaque recording the fact that Edward VII held a meeting of the Privy Council in this room in 1903. The *chapel*, originally designed by Brooks, was redecorated in marble early this century, and in the ante-chapel is the recumbent effigy of the 3rd Marquis. There has been a chaplain attached to Wynyard since 1454, and the chapel is in regular use. The lower south wing has been transformed into a family house by the present marquis—and the garden terrace surveys a beautiful prospect of the serpentine lake winding its way out of sight. At the highest point in the park stands the obelisk, which was erected to mark the visit of the Duke of Wellington in 1827. The Londonderrys have always been a great political family and Wynyard has been a great scene of political parties. Edward VII, George V, Edward VIII, George VI and the present Queen have all stayed here—as have the Duke of Wellington, Disraeli and Winston Churchill. In the 1920s and 1930s the wife of the 7th Marquis was the greatest political hostess in the country: daughter of Henry Chaplin, Edith Lady Londonderry was nicknamed 'Circe' because of her extraordinary power of fascinating all with whom she came in touch. Her friendship with Ramsay MacDonald (who was M.P. for Seaham Harbour) made him suspect among some of his supporters, who accused him of having forsaken 'the world of cloth caps for the society of tiaras and champagne'.

Index

Eastgate lead-mining relic